Pervasive Developmental Disorder

Pervasive Developmental Disorder
An Altered Perspective

Barbara Quinn and Anthony Malone

Jessica Kingsley Publishers
London and Philadelphia

First published in the United Kingdom in 2000 by
Jessica Kingsley Publishers Ltd
116 Pentonville Road,
London N1 9JB, England
and
325 Chestnut Street,
Philadelphia, PA19106, USA

www.jkp.com

Copyright © 2000 Barbara Quinn and Anthony Malone

Library of Congress Cataloging in Publication Data

A CIP catalog record for this book is available from the British Library

British Library Cataloguing in Publication Data

A CIP catalogue record for this book is available from the Library of Congress

ISBN 1 85302 876 2

Printed and Bound in Great Britain by
Athenaeum Press, Gateshead, Tyne and Wear

Contents

FOREWORD 7

ACKNOWLEDGEMENTS 8

ABOUT THE AUTHORS 9

Sam Likes Trains 11

Introduction 13

1 What is Pervasive Developmental Disorder? 17

2 Social Reciprocity 35

3 Communication 47

4 Impairment in Play Style 57

5 More Characteristics 63

6 The Evaluation Process 71

7 What Can Be Done? Medical Perspective 79

8 What Can Be Done? Educational Perspective 87

9 Additional Options 107

10 Up Close and Personal 111

RESOURCES 149

REFERENCES 151

INDEX 153

Foreword

In recent years, with the broadening diagnostic terminology in the field of Developmental Pediatrics and the increase in the number of children being diagnosed with Pervasive Developmental Disorder, Barbara Quinn and Anthony Malone found a need to provide families with appropriate reference material. Current materials referred more to the severe end of the spectrum and did not individualize the approach for each child.

Dr Malone and Mrs Quinn felt that the first step following the diagnosis of a developmental disorder is for the parent to have a full understanding of what the diagnosis means and how their child fits into that diagnostic terminology. Only then can they effectively move on to accept the diagnosis and proceed with implementing appropriate education and intervention for their child. This book is intended to educate and support families through the difficult process of answering *'What does this all mean?'* and *'Where do we go from here?'*

Acknowledgements

We would like to extend a very special thanks to the parents who shared their candid and genuine stories. Your spirit and commitment are truly inspirational! Parents are the energy beneath the flame of hope and their children are the glow above that flame. Our words can only say 'Thank you!' Your actions spell unconditional love and profound hope.

We would also like to thank the many professionals who shared their expertise with us, and more importantly, share it with children daily. Our gratitude goes out to Carol Winn for her valuable input and support of the project and to Ned Hoskins for his editorial assistance.

Personal Thanks from Barbara

My love and deep gratitude go to Charles and Rosalie Hunter who paved the way with love and joy. To my husband, Rick Quinn, who puts a smile in my heart every day and whose encouragement and support made this project possible. To my children, Patrick and Jennifer, my greatest blessings!

Personal Thanks from Anthony

To each and every child that has been part of my personal and professional experience, I offer the greatest of thanks for enriching my life.

About the Authors

Barbara L. Quinn brings to her writing 16 years of nursing experience. In her role as Nurse Clinician in Developmental Pediatrics at Albany Medical College, she works directly with families of children with Pervasive Developmental Disorder (PDD). Barbara is committed to educating parents and helping them to come to terms with what a developmental diagnosis means to both child and family. This book is an extension of her commitment to support those families.

As a freelance writer, Barbara has authored articles on child development and parenting issues. She has a graduate degree in Educational Psychology.

Barbara is the mother of two school-age children who, she states, provide her with her greatest lessons in child development as they share the incredible gifts of their childhood.

Anthony F. Malone is a pediatrician with a specialty in child development. In his 20 years of practice, he has worked with many families of children with a wide variety of developmental difficulties. As Director of the Division of Developmental and Behavioral Pediatrics at Albany Medical College, he wears many hats. In addition to evaluating children and making recommendations to families, he also has the responsibility of educating up and coming pediatricians and other professionals in the field.

In addition to his time spent at the Developmental Pediatric office, Dr Malone provides pediatric care to typical and special needs children in his active private practice. His expertise was recently recognized by selection to appear in the newly released guide, *The Best Doctors in America: Northeast Region.*

Dr Malone has much 'hands on' parenting experience and genuine appreciation for the challenges of parenting, as well as the joys.

Sam Likes Trains

The black and white creature appeared to be sucking his thumb, as the doctor pointed out the small beating heart. For Michelle and Rob this was a moment that they could never have imagined. The first ultrasound of their unborn child moved them to tears. With photos in hand they returned home that day with the security of knowing that their baby was 'just fine'.

The following months passed quickly and without much difficulty. Michelle gave up her morning coffee and actually counted the pieces of fruit she consumed each day. They explored the many baby departments and finally decided on a Pooh Bear theme for the nursery. While carefully aligning the wallpaper border on the center of the wall, Rob dreamed of his child, who would surely have intelligence, athletic prowess, and good looks.

The day arrived. With a combination of panic and excitement they headed for the hospital. Sam came into the world shrivelled up, cone-headed, and screaming, but was nothing short of absolutely beautiful to the eyes of his parents. Family came and 'cooed' at him, nurses fussed over him and, with the exception of the exhaustion Michelle felt, all was good in the world.

They arrived home within two days and Sam was given a tour of his special room. Stuffed animals adorned the shelves and the balloons painted on the wall appeared almost within reach from the crib. Tucked up in his crib, Sam fell asleep and his parents watched him, as he breathed in and out, in and out. Their baby was home.

Days turned into weeks and weeks into months. Sam rolled over as expected, crawled as expected and climbed onto Dad's lap into his awaiting embrace, as expected. He crawled through the house and discovered intriguing spots, such as Dad's tie rack with the multitude of colors hanging down. By his first birthday, he was walking and giggling and delighted at the sight of his birthday candles.

The following year brought changes for the family. A brother was born, but Michelle felt that Sam had hardly noticed him. The few words that Sam had spoken earlier hadn't been uttered recently. Thinking that this was related to the newcomer, Michelle and Rob vowed to spend more time with Sam, as surely this was all he needed. But their concerns grew. Their affectionate child now seemed content only to sit and play with the wheels of his train. Rob would set up the train on its track and Sam would watch it go around and around, and he would shake his arms and flap his hands with excitement.

The biggest concern that Michelle had, began to reveal itself more and more over time. It was Sam's speech. One Saturday morning during library circle time, Michelle watched from a distance as Sam repeatedly fanned a book with his fingers while the other children attentively watched puppets conclude their story. Eagerly raising their hands, the toddlers shared their impressions. 'Mom-mee Babbit!' said one youngster as he pointed at the animated sock. 'The Mommy rabbit won't let the baby rabbit run away,' shared another little girl. Michelle whispered to Sam, and then repeated his name in a louder voice, but Sam still didn't respond. The group disbanded and his mother joined Sam on the mat. Michelle put her child on her lap and began to look at a book with him. She tried to engage him in looking at the pictures and urged him to point to the objects on the pages, but Sam was more interested in the motion of fanning the remaining pages.

Later that night, Michelle shared her concerns with Rob. She suggested that perhaps Sam couldn't hear very well. Rob reassured Michelle that 'surely all little girls talk sooner than boys' and that Sam 'just gets very focused sometimes'. He reviewed with her that Sam was indeed talking. He could repeat the end of a sentence and could say some phrases out of his favorite video. Certainly, Sam was smart. He pulled his parents to the refrigerator when he wanted a drink; he was able to run a VCR, figure out the mixing bowl switches, and was fascinated by his trains. But even Rob noticed that Sam didn't consistently respond to his name being called, and he agreed that maybe his hearing did need to be tested.

Michelle was reassured for a while, but other issues kept cropping up renewing her concerns. When friends came to visit, Sam did not seem particularly interested in their arrival and Michelle became exasperated by the amount of supervision Sam needed. She couldn't leave him for a split second in case he became intrigued with the one thing he shouldn't be, like an appliance plug or the hairblower. She discovered that the only safe way to take a shower was to put in a 'Barney' tape and he would be certain to stare at that for as long as she allowed the tape to run.

Michelle and Rob found themselves discussing Sam's peculiarities often and arguing about their parenting styles. They eventually agreed that something was a little odd about Sam.

Introduction

To the Parent/Reader

Pervasive Developmental Disorder, not otherwise specified (PDD, NOS), is the diagnostic terminology used to define children who present along an expansive continuum of impairments. These children share, in common, impairments in the areas of communication, socialization, and a restricted repertoire of play. The degree of impairment a child has in any given area, however, greatly influences its individual developmental picture. We are hopeful that this book will further explain how your individual child may or may not fit this diagnostic picture.

This was a hard book to write due to the subject matter, the expanding diagnostic terminology and the desire to serve the individual needs of each child and family. Because children with Pervasive Developmental Disorder (PDD) present along a wide spectrum of difficulties, it is hard to perceive of these children sharing the same umbrella term of diagnosis. It is imperative that we look at each child as an individual with a unique developmental presentation. Every child presents as a wonderfully complicated collection of strengths, perhaps with some delays and/or deficits. The child is further individualized by his or her own personality, temperament, and world around them. Taking all these factors into account makes it difficult to understand how we can developmentally classify children at all. However, professionals in this field can be very helpful in accurately assessing these factors and in providing diagnostic information and guidance. Use of developmental diagnosis when a child presents with a particular collection of characteristics, is important in helping us direct our intervention and attention. The value of 'putting a name' on the struggles that a child faces helps us focus our energies to optimize the child's development.

How to read this book

Some of the information on the following pages will apply to your child, and some will not. Use the information that is meaningful to you. It might be helpful to go to a chapter that particularly looks at your area of concern for your child and read that first. For example, if your main area of concern has been in the language area, you may want to brief the chapter on communication and review the characteristics of language that are apparent in children with PDD. If you feel a need to hear another parent's story before getting into the more technical issues involved in PDD, you may want to begin by reading Chapter 10: *Up Close and Personal.* This book does not need to be read from the beginning to the end, or in a particular order. Below is a brief overview of the contents of the chapters in this book, to assist you in finding information that is most relevant to you and your child. It is presented to help you best reference and utilize the enclosed information.

Note: Generally when the term PDD is used in this text, it is intended to mean PDD, NOS.

CHAPTER I

This chapter is an extensive review of the areas of impairment associated with PDD. It is an attempt to encapsulate and explain the complexity and nature of the disorder. Learning about the basics of the disorder may be a good place to start for some. Likewise, it may be overwhelming and confusing for others. If you find it so, progress to other parts of the book for clarification, and then return to Chapter 1 again at a later time. It is not important to have a complete understanding of the contents of Chapter 1 before moving on. The points addressed are reviewed in detail and clarified in subsequent chapters.

CHAPTER 2

A descriptive story is offered at the beginning of Chapter 2 that looks at a likely display of the altered social style of children with PDD. The chapter goes on to further explain typical development of social skills and how these skills are altered in the child with PDD. It looks at the wide range of presentations and concludes with addressing some frequently asked questions.

CHAPTER 3

The power of communication is addressed in this chapter. Both non-verbal and verbal communication is discussed. Typical development of speech and language is reviewed to set a basis for comparison. Some definitions and differences in communication style seen with PDD are given and frequently asked questions are answered.

CHAPTER 4

Descriptive stories relating to play schemes offers insight into the differences seen in the play repertoire of the child with PDD. The spectrum, or range, of impairment is addressed and frequently asked questions are answered.

CHAPTER 5

In this chapter, additional characteristics associated with PDD are reviewed. These include sensory perception, alterations in motor skills, physical mannerisms, and unusual strengths.

CHAPTER 6

This chapter walks through the process of having a child's development evaluated. It reviews the professionals who might be involved in such a process and what role is taken by the various specialists.

CHAPTER 7

In Chapter 7, an attempt is made to answer the very important question of 'What can be done?' The medical approach to interventions and treatments is defined.

CHAPTER 8

This chapter continues in the efforts to look at *'What can be done?'* by specifically addressing educational perspectives and methods. Chapters 7 and 8 are intended to give an overview of options and a preliminary understanding of the multiple methods of intervention strategies currently being employed with children with PDD.

CHAPTER 9

A brief review of additional options is discussed including discussion on *alternative therapies,* use of the Internet, and support groups.

CHAPTER 10

Parents generously share their stories. These personal accounts provide insight into the disorder and offer support. They most certainly communicate that you are not alone in battling with the struggles associated with PDD.

It is our hope that after reading this book, you will have an understanding of some key issues associated with PDD. Additionally, it is our hope that after reading this book you will have a better understanding of your individual child and of how to proceed in promoting his/her development.

Key points

- ◦ PDD is a diagnostic way of viewing the developmental style of a child.
- ◦ PDD is caused by a physical difference in the brain function of the child. Nobody caused this difference!
- ◦ Every child is a unique and special individual.
- ◦ The diagnosis does not define the child. The child's developmental presentation and the diagnosis help us understand some underlying struggles.
- ◦ Interventions focused on specific areas of impairment can have a profound impact.
- ◦ **It is a bright future!**

CHAPTER I

What is Pervasive Developmental Disorder?

What is typical development?

Before we can have a thorough understanding of what a developmental disorder is, we need to have an understanding of *typical*, often referred to as 'normal', development. Perhaps nothing is more interesting to the human species than the understanding of ourselves and how we grow. Child development has been studied from many viewpoints including the fields of education, medicine, sociology, and psychology. One need only explore the local bookstore to discover the multitude of volumes on the many facets of growth and development. One can conclude, from any perspective taken, that typical development is most simply defined as *healthy development, a progressive process that follows along a course of expected outcomes.*

The expectations of progress in healthy development are based on information obtained from observations and studies of a large number of children in a given age range. Appropriate developmental progress and stages are determined by establishing the commonalties in age groups. When observing a group of one-year-old children, one is witness to some very inquisitive little human creatures who are very interested in exploring and getting around. Some may be walking independently, while others manage the terrain with the assistance of handy props, such as chairs and coffee tables. The one-year-old curiosity is the stimulating factor that assists in the learning of motor milestones. Furthermore, these little ones may have a few words, or they may not, but be certain that they are able to make their needs known! Whether it is a preference of juice over milk or a desire to go out for a walk, the one-year-old has already established a relatively sophisticated system of communicating with their caregiver. The use of facial expressions, gestures, different crying tones and qualities are all means of communication that are intact in the one-year-old.

It is to be noted that there is a good deal of variation in typical development. Children are not frozen in a moment of time but rather develop over many years, therefore, it is only reasonable that there are variations of the onset of given skills from child to child. One need only look at a nursery school classroom of children to see that 'Susie' may be speaking in complete sentences while 'Johnny' only has a few words. Additionally, personality and individual strengths and weaknesses play into the acquisition of healthy developmental skills.

How does personality effect development?

Let us not forget that children are people after all, and have many things that set them apart from one another. Individuality, our expression of ourselves, is innate to humanity. Our personalities and temperamental qualities certainly influence how we grow and learn. A naturally gregarious infant may smile at the mother walking by, while a more serious baby studies the mother's face for a long period of time before rewarding her with a grin. Individual aptitudes also need to be factored into the various presentations of healthy development. Aptitudes, or innate abilities, are those skills that come easily to one child, yet may be difficult for another. Janice could take piano lessons and practice diligently for several years, but she may still never become a concert pianist. Kevin, on the other hand, may study piano for the same amount of time, find it easy, and some day find his fingers gracing the ivories at Carnegie Hall! Kevin has an *aptitude* for music.

Personality and aptitudes may influence the rate in which some skills are mastered, but these individual qualities do not greatly alter the course of development *unless these qualities are extreme.* Personality and temperamental qualities all contribute to healthy development as long as the personal characteristics are within the range of 'normal'. It is not until they are extreme or out of the typical range that they effect learning, socialization, and overall functioning of life skills.

MARY

Mary, a timid child, entered a birthday party and smiled sheepishly at the sight of the balloons and at her girlfriends. She clung to her mother's leg and hesitated in joining the fun. Once she 'warmed up', she quietly joined in the festivities. Though she never became chatty with her friends, she was certainly able to let the hostess know that she wanted chocolate icecream with her cake.

A shy temperament has not altered Mary's development to the point of severely influencing her understanding of the communication process, or her awareness of what is going on around her. However, being *extremely shy*, to the point of becoming fearful and being unable to interact at all appropriately, may indeed lead to an altered path of development in the area of speech and language and/or socialization.

ELIZABETH

Elizabeth, an extremely shy child, entered a birthday party and became filled with anxiety and fear. She was unable to release the grasp of her mother's thigh. She could not look around the room or engage in any interaction with the other party-goers. Eventually, the mother made excuses and left the party. The child felt no disappointment, but rather relief.

Demonstrating this extreme of a temperamental characteristic, in this illustration, shyness may influence the course of that child's social development. Social skills, like all skills, require practice. Play situations, like birthday parties, are the social classroom of the child. If anxiety prevents such interaction, it is reasonable to think that it will alter the path to how a child learns to socialize.

There are many temperamental qualities which flavor a child's development. Emotionality, or how a child wears his or her emotions, varies hugely in healthy development. 'Sally' may jubilantly embrace her aunt while 'Cody' smiles tentatively at her outstretched arms. To further illustrate this, if Sally greeted complete strangers at the Mall the same way she greeted her aunt, or if Cody ran to hide in the closet every time someone came to the door, one might become concerned about how the child's way of expressing feeling and emotions will impact his or her development. Think of all the personality characteristics of people and the range of presentations; enthusiastic to overly energetic, inquisitive to pensive, cheerful to exuberant, motivated to driven. The list could go on and on. While these characteristics alter the style of a child's development, or flavor the nature of the child, they do not significantly impact developmental progression, unless they are presented to the extreme.

Can personality differences be a good thing?

The answer to this question is, of course, a resounding 'Yes!' Differences among people not only add flavor to life, but fulfil the multiple needs of human beings. We need electricians, painters, doctors, and teachers (to name only a few) and there are unlikely to be many people who could fit all of these roles. We certainly need to embrace the individuality of any child and foster the strengths they present to us.

History reveals to us several people who were felt perhaps to have extreme temperamental qualities, which today, and in some cases in their day as well, caused them to be viewed as significantly different. Included among those were some great thinkers and creators. Picasso was criticized for having such a different perspective of the world, but his unique perspective gave us the gift of his beautiful art. Albert Einstein was also ridiculed for his unusual way of looking at the world and his desire not to follow the *status quo*. He contributed a tremendous amount of knowledge of our world by having an altered perspective. History recounts the lives of several men and women who failed to fit the mold of expected social norms, or who failed to take the accepted vantage point, and yet they left behind gifts that have extended well beyond their lifetimes.

There seems to be today, a heightened awareness of the need to foster the individual strengths of children. It is becoming more acceptable to embrace the differences in children and even more importantly, to facilitate learning and overall school progress by truly accepting that no two people are educationally, socially or creatively equal!

No parent wants to have a child fall out of the domain of the norm. It's a rough road to hoe when behaviors and learning styles are so different that a child needs specialized help and attention. Yet we are reminded by Picasso, Einstein, and others, that perhaps coloring outside of the lines, or looking at something from an unusual angle has great value! How did we come to know that the world was not flat?

What is a developmental delay?

As mentioned, healthy development follows along a predictable path. When a child is obtaining developmental skills along the predicted path but more slowly than expected, they are said to be *delayed.* For the purpose of illustration, let's look at a car-ride. Our destination is 60 miles away and we can go between 45 mph and 60 mph. That means that our estimated time of arrival is somewhere between 1 and 1½ hours. This represents normal development. In the case of delayed development, the car does not change its course, but arrives 2 to 3 hours after the expected time. Let us apply this concept to child development. If a child moved its total body as an infant, but was a little slow to sit independently, and did not walk until close to 16 months of age, one could say that this child is progressing at a slower pace than his/her peers. This progress is not different. It is just *delayed.*

What is a developmental disorder?

When we speak of a difference in the pattern or nature of the developmental process, we are speaking of a *disorder.* Categorizing into groups those behaviors or differences that set some children apart from their peers defines a *developmental disorder.* A well-known developmental disorder is Attention Deficit Hyperactive Disorder (ADHD). Children with this disorder have in common, the inability to focus their attention appropriately and they have a high degree of physical activity. They have a common group of characteristics that are different from their peers, yet similar to each other. Therefore, ADHD is said to be a *developmental disorder.*

Children with developmental disorders are not merely slow in obtaining skills. Applying this case to the concept above, children with developmental disabilities are not travelling at a slower pace, they are travelling a different route all together. They may arrive at the same point, but they will need some help and guidance along the way. They either have a different way of acquiring appropriate developmental skills than expected, or they have a lessened capacity of acquiring certain skills.

What is Pervasive Developmental Disorder?

Pervasive Developmental Disorder (PDD) is the diagnostic terminology for a group of individuals who present with an underlying impairment in the communication process and connectedness to the world around them. This impairment in turn *pervades* over all areas of development. The inability to fully connect, or relate appropriately to ones' surroundings greatly influences learning and the pathway of development. As mentioned previously, a developmental disorder entails a compilation of characteristics that set the group apart from their peers but are in common with each other. In the case of PDD, the characteristics include impairments in the areas of *language and communication, socialization, and use of imaginative play.* The disorder is viewed as a *spectrum disorder* because there is a great deal of variability in the presentation of the disorder along a spectrum of severity. Therefore, the diagnostic terminology of Pervasive Developmental Disorder (PDD) is an umbrella term that encompasses a continuum of impairments in communication, socialization, and play repertoire.

Terms used within this framework are Asperger Syndrome; PDD, not otherwise specified (NOS); and autism. These all represent different degrees of impairment along a continuum. The areas which are effected, although to differing degrees, are shared.

To elaborate on this spectrum concept, let us look specifically at the range of impairment in each area. In the area of language and communication, a child's abilities may range from one who is able to verbalize well and communicate ideas and thoughts clearly, to one who has no language at all. Impairment in the social realm can range from being slightly distant and described as aloof, to one who has no direct eye contact or response to their surroundings. Play skills can vary greatly from a child who plays with toys as if they are symbolic of real life, to one who plays mechanically with the movable parts of a favored toy.

It is clear to see how differently any two children on this spectrum of disorders may present. One child may use language to request his food preference at a meal, meet your face to seek assistance, and play rowboat on the log outside. Another may use no words, have only fleeting eye contact and spend playtime spinning the wheels of a toy truck. As illustrated, these two children have significantly different degrees of impairment, however, they are on the same spectrum of disorder.

The degrees of impairment in communication, socialization, and play style greatly alter the ultimate course of development. PDD represents a different pathway of development, or a different pattern of thinking and perspective, than that of a typical child. This altered perspective impacts the developmental course. In order for the diagnostic terminology to apply, all three areas must be effected to some degree, across the broad spectrum.

The particular components of PDD will be more fully addressed in later chapters. For the purpose of understanding the diagnostic terminology the important thing to keep in mind is that there is a *qualitative difference* in the development of the process of communication, socialization, and repertoire of play. By looking at these qualitative differences in the development of these children, we are able to look at the individual child and take their own strengths and weaknesses into account. This allows us to set up the most appropriate intervention and educational plan for each child and optimize that individual child's potential.

In addition to impairments in communication, socialization, and play style, often children with PDD have other characteristics as well. These include differences of sensory perceptions, physical mannerisms, and unusual strengths. The presentation of these characteristics differs greatly from one child to the next. Altered perception of sensory input may cause a child to see, feel, or hear things differently to that which others might experience. For this reason they may respond unexpectedly to sensory input. They may demonstrate only minor sensory difficulties or they may be intolerant to certain noises, sources of lights, food textures, or the feel of particular clothing fabrics. Sometimes children with PDD are even fussy about the tags in their shirts or having their sleeves rolled up, or down. A child who does not even flinch when his/her name is called 10 times, may head for the window at the sound of an ambulance siren in the far distance. Each child may present with their own nuances, as we all do, and alone they may mean nothing. When put together collectively, however, they characterize PDD. Sensory processing differences, and struggles with intolerance of particular stimuli can effect the overall functional level of the child.

Unusual movements, or *mannerisms*, are also associated with this disorder. It is common for the child with PDD to have an unusual gait, hand movements, head movements, or other peculiar body movements. Hand flapping and rocking are often seen and felt to be *self-stimulating behaviors*. These behaviors somehow cause an internal response in the child that reinforces itself and therefore the child repeats it. To watch some of these mannerisms can be very distressing for parents, as they are visible outward signs of the internal differences in the development of their child.

Another characteristic seen in children with PDD is the presentation of unusual strengths. Early reading, or *hyperlexia*, is somewhat common among these children. Some have very good abilities with puzzles, demonstrating skills in spatial relations beyond their age expectation. Exceptional memory skills, such as the ability to recite an entire dialogue from their favorite video, may be exhibited. Children with PDD may also acquire depths of knowledge on given topics well beyond what one would expect for their age. Also, advanced technical musical skills may be part of this more pleasant side of a baffling disorder.

Secondary diagnosis

Children with PDD can have secondary medical and/or psychiatric problems that contribute to their difficulties and developmental struggles. One such concurrent diagnosis is *Attention Deficit Hyperactive Disorder (ADHD)*. The core concern is that over-activity, impulse control problems and inattentiveness have deleterious effects on learning and functioning. This includes learning and 'tuning in' to social skills and communication skills which are at the crux of the problems for the child with PDD.

Obsessive/Compulsive Disorder (OCD) can be seen in conjunction with PDD and is so often a part of the lives of these children that it can actually be one of the determining factors in the diagnosis. OCD is a psychiatric disorder characterized by repetitive thought and subsequent repetitive actions that are not particularly useful and in most cases obstruct normal learning and functioning. Parents have reported such circumstances as a child having to turn the television on and off exactly 14 times before he or she is able to leave the room. Another reports a child who upon entering his house *has* to watch the washing machine spin for an extended period of time before he is able to even take his coat off. Some children with PDD struggle with only aspects of OCD, while others are more significantly impaired by this condition.

Anxiety disorders may be seen with children with PDD. Anxiety is experienced by all children to some extent but it becomes a disorder when the physical and emotional response is so intense and unpleasant to the child that it impairs his/her functioning. The apprehension the child feels is not in synch with the stimulus of fear. For example, a child with an anxiety disorder and PDD may be so uncomfortable around the sound of rollerblades on a rink that upon entering just the parking lot of the arena he begins to shout, rock and sweat. The children may even have anxiety in circumstances that have no precipitant. They may experience severe internal stress for unknown, or undeniable reasons.

Sleep disorder is yet another secondary manifestation of PDD. Lacking the internal mechanism to calm and comfort themselves, many of these children have difficulty falling asleep, and/or staying asleep through the night.

What is Asperger Syndrome?

JOHN GOES TO KINDERGARTEN

It was only the second week of the school year, but the children had begun to settle into their school-day routine. John followed his classmates off the bus and into his classroom without responding to the greetings of his principal and teacher along the way. He dutifully put his things away in his assigned cubicle and proceeded to line up his pencils in a perfect row. This was a ritual he had taken to daily. John covered his ears to the sound of the school bell. His teacher approached him, turned him to face her, and quietly redirected him to the gathering area. He joined the other children on the rug and was interested in what the teacher had in store for them that day. He is an eager learner, particularly if it is an area of special interest to him, like dinosaurs or puzzles. His friend, Jenny, sat down next to him and he noticed the pink ribbon hanging from her pigtail. He began to bat at the ribbon and laughed as it began to swing back and forth. He stroked her ponytail and playfully pulled it. 'John pulled my hair!' Jenny yelled as she ran towards the teacher. The teacher reminded John to keep his hands to himself and he looked puzzled as Jenny found another spot in which to sit.

The lesson began with a review of the day of the week, the month of the year, and plans for the school day. The teacher eventually got to John's favorite topic, the weather. Unable to restrain himself from interrupting this time, he began to recite to pattern of *Hurricane Hortense*. Imitating the inflections of the weather man, John reiterated the hurricane's course, speed of the winds, volume of moisture and amounts of precipitation. Delighting in his depth of knowledge on the topic, his teacher prodded him with questions. 'What happened to the land and buildings after the hurricane hit, John?' 'How do you think the people felt after they lost their homes?' she asked. John initially looked somewhat baffled by her questions and then returned to his telecast of the 120-mile winds.

The fall season progressed and John became more and more acclimatized to the school routines. He followed his peers lead now and began to copy their mannerisms and reactions in certain situations. He established a friendship with a boy who loved to run a lot and climb in the playground. They enjoyed each other's company and though John could be a little clumsy, he had no fear of climbing and jumping on or off anything. He learned the rules for kick ball and adhered to them rigidly. He got very confused when the other children squabbled over missing the bases or being out. He had difficulty relating to most of the children and began to recognize that.

In the classroom, John revealed himself to be a bright boy with exceptional skills in maths and with puzzles. He was also able to read above age expectation, though he did not demonstrate a good understanding of what he had read. His teacher wondered how to meet his needs. In some ways he seemed advanced, yet in others he was immature. His teacher found him gifted in some respects. She also found him a little 'odd'.

John represents a child with Asperger Syndrome. *Asperger Syndrome (AS)* is a mild form of Pervasive Developmental Disorder. Professionals continue to debate whether AS is actually on the spectrum of PDD or is an entirely separate diagnosis. Some feel AS is synonymous with High Functioning Autism (HFA) while others feel that they are separate diagnoses. When considering this issue in terms of what they actually mean to the child, it becomes apparent that the differentiating of these diagnoses does not have a lot of practical application. The important point at hand is that the difficulties in communication and socialization are shared and those are the areas that need to be specifically addressed. Children with AS, who have generally intact language and learning skills, can grow to live independently and have productive lives. It is felt that for most individuals, even those minimally effected, there is always some degree of social dysfunction present. When given the adequate tools as a child, however, in adulthood they are able to use those tools for the necessities of socialization. Daily living requires us to be connected to the people and world around us, to understand the social mores, or social rules of our society, and to be able to interact effectively to get our needs met and desires known.

Hans Asperger, a Viennese physician (the origin of the disorder's name), recognized this disorder in the 1940s (Frith 1991). Interestingly, even though it was discovered quite some time ago, it has only recently been a universally recognized developmental disorder in the United States. In 1994 the criteria for diagnosis was clearly established in the *Diagnostic and Statistical Manual of Mental Disorders, 4th edn* (DSM-IV), a manual used by professionals in the field that outlines standard guidelines for mental and developmental diagnoses (American Psychiatric Association [APA]1994).

Language development in children with Asperger Syndrome is generally intact and this contributes to the high functional level of these children as compared to children more severely inflicted on the Pervasive Developmental Disorder spectrum. Slightly more inflicted children on the spectrum may be *echolalic*, or repeat what is said, rather than create their own thoughts and sentences. They may repeat parts of a sentence or reiterate entire passages from a television commercial. As they develop language it may have an unusual *prosody*, or tone and rhythm quality. Varying intonations and inflections present as a 'sing-song' quality of speech. When they are older they have useful speech, but often they remain very concrete in their thinking and communicating. One child with Asperger Syndrome asked his mother why the car had bounced after riding over a bump. The mother answered, 'There was a depression in the road.' The boy responded, 'Why is the road sad?'

Social interactions are characterized by one-sided approaches to communication and rather bizarre interactions. Like John illustrates above, children with Asperger Syndrome are unable to pick up on non-verbal cues and the subtleties of changes in facial expressions, body language, and other forms of unspoken communication. Due to this, and perhaps because they are sometimes coined as odd by their peers, they have a difficult time making emotional connections to peers and establishing friendships. They may then have fewer opportunities to practice social skills. Tuning in to the child with Asperger Syndrome and helping to develop good social skills is very much facilitated by the clear understanding of the disorder and early emphasis on the specific areas of difficulty for the child.

What is autism?

ALEX IN THE SAND BOX

'Want to go outside, Alex?' Mary yelled from the kitchen. After no response, she headed to the family room to check on her son. Alex sat in the rocker swaying back and forth. Mary grabbed the arms of the chair to slow the rocking pace and to try to get her son's attention. Alex began to hum in what had almost become a chant to his parents. It seemed whenever Alex got excited he would make these unusual noises. 'Alex, do you want to go outside?' she repeated as she took his angelic face in her hands and tried to look into his eyes. Alex briefly looked at his mom but she did not get the impression that he was actually seeing her. He quickly diverted his gaze and began to flap his hands.

Eventually, after more verbal attempts to get her child to respond to her, Mary physically led her child to the porch door. Though not resisting her efforts, Alex did not show any particular interest in the idea of going outside. Once he saw the screen door, however, he began to squeal and repeatedly moved the door on its hinges until his mother prompted him towards the sandbox. Again, Alex squealed as he began to run the sand through his hands. Despite the presence of toys and tools to play with in the sandbox, Alex ran his hands through the sand watching it spill over his fingers. He seemed to be in his own little world.

Alex represents a child with *autism*. Autism is the most serious form of Pervasive Developmental Disorder. The three characteristics of PDD; communication, social reciprocity and a restricted view of the world are all significantly affected in children with autism. There

must be significant interaction problems and disordered communication for autism to be considered diagnostically.

Pervasive Developmental Disorder is also referred to as within *the
autistic spectrum*, because children within the spectrum share the same
areas of impairment as those with true autism. The relatively new
diagnostic terminology in the field has led to some inconsistencies in
the use of the terms PDD and autism. Some professionals feel that
autism is autism alone and they continue to use this diagnosis to cover
quite a range of developmental disorder. One need only compare the
two given examples of John and Alex to see the great degree of
difference in the presentation of these two children. Though both
exhibit deficits in socialization skills, communication skills, and use
of imaginative play, their degree of functioning is significantly
different. By looking at PDD as a spectrum, it allows us to define
more clearly each child's individual developmental picture.

The first description of autism was defined by Leo Kanner in
1943 (Frith 1991, p.93). At that time, he believed the collected
characteristics of this group of children to be unique and specific.
These children were further defined under the general label of
childhood psychosis or childhood schizophrenia. The cause of this
disorder at that time was thought to be the *refrigerator mom*: a mother
who was so cold and withdrawn from her infant that she in fact
caused her child not to connect fully to the world around them. It
didn't take long, however, for professionals to realize that this was
simply not the case. After much observation of mothers and their
autistic children, it was concluded that perhaps the cause of their
developmental differences was something inherent in the child. We
have come a long way in our thinking. It is universally recognized
that some sort of neurologic dysfunction, or the system of the brain
not working just right, is the cause of these disorders.

What is PDD (NOS)?

TOM GOES SHOPPING

Tom's mother Sally headed to the grocery store to pick up a few
things. She preferred not to bring Tom along due to the trials that

arose, but today she had no choice. Seated in the back seat of the car the four-year-old cheerfully played with his bus. 'Vroom, vroom,' he said as he pushed the bus back and forth on the seat beside his. Sally took an unusual route today to drop a check off at the bank. 'Go to store!' Tom exclaimed from that back seat. 'Yes, we're going to the store but I have to go a different way today' she answered calmly. She knew that this change of course might set off a tantrum so she immediately put in his favorite Sesame Street cassette and he sang along as she completed her errand and headed on to the store.

He took her hand as they crossed the parking lot and sat in the shopping cart without resistance. 'Tom, Tom,' he said while pointing to the soda machines on the way in. 'Do you want a soda, Tom?' his mother asked already knowing the answer, as every time they came to the store he got a soda. 'Tom, Tom,' he repeated adamantly pointing toward the machine. Sally gave him some coins and he deposited them and selected his drink.

While waiting at the deli, Tom ran his finger around the surface on the rim of the soda can. He studied the droplets of water that had formed on the can as they drizzled down the sides. Sally handed him his bus but he was uninterested in that now. He maintained his attention on the droplets. Sally had noticed him slip into the place within himself that he often went, so she attempted to engage him in the here and now. 'Tom, how about we get some turkey for our picnic tomorrow?' she asked. 'Picnic tomorrow.' Tom repeated. He looked at his mother's face and smiled. 'You like to go on picnics, don't you Tom?' She attempted to extend their conversation. Tom smiled and clapped.

Tom represents a child with *PDD (NOS)*. It is easy to see that a lot of children fall between, or have varying behavioral patterns, from the two extremes on the spectrum of Pervasive Developmental Disorder: Asperger Syndrome and autism. The term *Pervasive Develop-mental Disorder, NOS (not otherwise specified)* is used to describe the children who are somewhere on the continuum of qualitative impair-ments in speech and communication, socialization, and repertoire of play. In the case of Tom, it is clear that he had some useful communication both with his words and gesturing, yet it is different to that which one would expect of a four-year-old. Also, he demonstrated a good amount of connection to his world, he related to his mother and was able to have eye contact, but he did recede into himself and it was sometimes an effort to engage him. Though he had a toy, he preferred to play with the droplets of water that ran down the soda can. Again, he had some minimal play skills, but they were not fully developed for his age. He was not as verbally adept, *per se*, as a child with Asperger Syndrome perhaps, nor did he reflect autism completely. He does share, in common with those two disorders, however, impairments in the areas of language, communication, and play repertoire. He is a child who falls on the spectrum of PDD but is not specifically at either end. He is said to be PDD, not otherwise specified (NOS).

Do we need to label children with PDD?

Parents are very concerned about the *labeling* of their child, and rightly so. A false label or mis-diagnosis may set the child on a course of intervention that is not appropriate for the given child. Also, parents fear the repercussions of the stigma of their child carrying a diagnosis associated with the spectrum of autism. One cannot deny that people have a preconceived notion of what autism is and even today some health professionals and educators are not familiar with the latest in terminology and thinking in this field. This puts the parent in the position of educating the people in their child's world as to what is the particular developmental picture of their child and what would likely be best for them. Let us remember that parents are the experts in their child's learning and play style. Professionals in the field of developmental pediatrics are there for the purpose of helping parents and their children to more clearly define areas of concern and to direct them onto the right path for the appropriate medical work-up, educational approach, and referral to any other necessary supports.

Looking at Pervasive Developmental Disorder as a spectrum and specifically defining each child's individual strengths and weaknesses is essential in establishing the right path and intervention for each child. Hopefully, with education and improved awareness, there will not be such a stigma associated with the terminology of a spectrum of autism and labeling won't be such an intimidating issue for families.

A recap

Differentiation of Asperger Syndrome; Pervasive Developmental Disorder, not otherwise specified; Autism.

Key characteristics of Asperger Syndrome

- Limitation in social interaction expressed by difficulty with peer relationships, non-verbal communication, interaction and interest in others, and expression of emotion.

- Restricted areas of interest and/or play. Presents as preoccupation or particular focus on subject to the exclusion of broader play schemes or diverse interests.

- Typical development of language and generally normal intelligence.

- Can include inflexibility with routines and rituals, physical mannerisms, preoccupations, and unusual strengths (such as early reading).

Key characteristics of Pervasive Developmental Disorder, not otherwise specified (PDD, NOS)

- Impairment in socialization seen in relationships and interactions with others.

- Impairment in communication seen as difficulties with non-verbal and verbal language. May have unusual speech patterns and use of words.

- Restricted repertoire of play and difficulties in applying the social world to their play schemes.

- May demonstrate some rigidity to change and inflexibility.

- ○ May present with unusual movements, sensory issues, motor difficulties, and perseverations.

Generally fewer and less serious presentations of these characteristics are seen with PDD, NOS than are seen with autism.

Key characteristics of autism

- ○ Severe impairment in eye contact, social connection and social interaction
- ○ Severe impairment in communication skill development inclusive of difficulties with non-verbal and verbal language.
- ○ Restricted repertoire of play and significant limitation in social play.
- ○ May have unusual repetitive movements or mannerisms.
- ○ May not have normal intelligence.

CHAPTER 2

Social Reciprocity

Social reciprocity is our natural understanding of how we relate to the people in the world around us. It is not clearly understood what brain processes are responsible for this innate connection to our fellow human beings which develops as we grow to a very sophisticated understanding of social nuances and social rules.

WILL YOU PLAY WITH ME, JASON?

The cool day did little to deter the preschoolers from playing in the playground on the first day of spring. The 'Mother's Day Out' group was gathering for their weekly get-together in which they enjoyed sharing their parenting tales and lamenting on the challenges of parenting. Though not spoken of, they also gathered to assess the behaviors and skills of the other children in the group. The information obtained from such observations proved to be both reassuring and provoking. It was comforting to exchange stories of how to manage 'terrible twos' tantrums and to join in laughs regarding failed attempts at 'time outs'. Yet for Karen, the afternoons shared with the other mothers and their children often left her confused and insecure. Though seldom mentioned by the others, her child, Peter, baffled them all. Peter always enjoyed his time with the group and Karen sometimes wondered why, as he seemed awkward and frustrated while trying to get the attention of the other children. But without fail, before the next time they were to get together, Peter would get excited and talk of his friends.

On this particular spring day, the mothers assumed their positions on the raised bench and sighed with the first gulps of their coffee. Peter had joined the kids running from the car to the playground but as they enthusiastically ventured to their desired play areas, Peter just looked on. Some of the children scurried to the large sandbox and began to shovel and pile and shovel some more. Tommy ran to get his toy truck and hurried back to his place next to Carl, who had already begun to construct an integrated town of curving roads. The two boys exchanged glances and 'vrooms' as they maneuvered their cars through the construction site. Jessica and Sarah looked on with little enthusiasm and with questioning facial expressions they communicated to each other their lack of interest in the boys' play scheme. Hand in hand they walked away to the tunnel. They were barely inside the tube when giggles could be heard and soon the tunnel was a pretend McDonald's drive-through. After taking Sarah's order for french fries, Jessica pretended to serve the treat and collect the money. When Melissa came upon the scene she observed the play from a slight distance. It took Melissa a while to warm up in a social setting and, though very interested in joining the other girls, she held back from them. Jessica, always the extrovert, saw her and yelled over. 'Wanna play Melissa?' The welcoming brought Melissa in line for a burger and fries. Despite being a shy child, Melissa readily took on her role.

Peter walked by the tunnel and looked on briefly. He stuck his head in the tunnel and was face to face with Sarah, their noses nearly touching. Sarah bolted backwards to achieve some personal space and looked at Peter inquisitively. Peter ran from the tunnel. Other children had chosen to play a game of tag and began running and climbing the various obstacles of the playground maze. As one boy tagged another, Peter looked on. The sandbox caught Peter's attention and he joined Carl and Tommy there. He made no conversation with them as he sat down and for a brief while he was content to move a toy car back and forth in the sand. He looked at Carl and Tommy and wanted badly to be a part of their play. While nudging Tommy, Peter began to recite the layout of the wheels on a fourteen-wheeler truck '...with vertical suspension and balanced axles…' He again nudged Tommy who had inched away from him. This time it caused Tommy to fall over on his side in the sand. He quickly righted himself and told Peter to stop pushing. Tommy positioned himself closer to Carl and resumed his play ignoring Peter. Peter sat still in the sand. He knew that the other boys were not interested in his story about the truck but he did not understand. They were playing trucks after all.

Squeals of delight, once again, echoed from the tunnel and Peter's attention was diverted to the girls' play. He ran to the tunnel and began to bang on the sides. Loud clashes resonated inside the tunnel sending Jessica and Sarah running out with fear on their faces. When they saw Peter and realized he had been the cause of the loud intrusion, they looked at each other and then at him. 'Peter!' They exclaimed in harmony. 'Stop it!' They ran off together to the swings. Peter heard Sarah say, 'He's always such a pill!' 'I just wanted to play,' he thought.

Again standing alone, Peter could not decide quite what he wanted to do. He began to play with the pebbles on the ground when some bigger boys went running by. Peter quickly started to chase the older children. They ignored his attempt to be part of their game, but Peter was happy just running after them almost without direction.

This is an example of how a child on the milder end of the Pervasive Developmental Disorder spectrum may interact in a social setting. Peter's social skills are characterized by a desire to socialize with his peers, attempts to interact with other children and to be a part of their play schemes, and an attempt to share a common interest with another child. These could be considered age-appropriate social skills except that in Peter's case, there is a developmental difference exhibited. Peter's social skills reflect an inability to fully understand the ingredients of appropriate social interaction for his age. He lacks perceptiveness of social nuances. His approaches to other children are often physical in nature, such as pushing Tommy or banging the tunnel, and he does not know how to effectively initiate interaction with other children. He demonstrates a poor understanding of the unspoken rules of body space, in other words, he invades other children's 'personal space'. Though he initiates conversation, it is not for the purpose of an exchange of ideas but rather more a recitation of factual information. Again, he does not instinctively know how to open a social interaction (i.e. 'What are you guys doing? Can I play with you?') or continuing a conversation, (i.e. reciting the facts about the truck structure). Peter has an *impairment in the area of social reciprocity*.

Social development in the first and second year

A young infant begins the process of social development by visually regarding the faces of his/her caregivers. Young infants demonstrate a preference to look at faces over colorful objects or moving mobiles. This initial establishment of eye contact becomes the basis of social skills. At a very early age, an infant will respond to various facial expressions. Surprisingly, a young baby can show signs of distress when a person looks at them with an angry or hostile expression. Soon the baby is able to elicit facial responses from another. Not only is he/she capable of reading the expression of another, but they understand that they have the ability to influence another person's facial response. This 'reading' of facial expressions continues to progress and at less than one year of age, babies are known to become distressed if their mother or father is crying or upset.

As social development continues, a baby comes to understand that he/she is a separate, independent, human being. Up until this point, they sense that they are a part of their primary care provider. An 8–11-month-old baby may become distressed when expecting to be separated from the parent, often to the point of screaming and sticking as much as possible to the chest of their mother. Much has been written about this occurrence, which is known as *separation anxiety*. This can be a difficult issue for child and parent alike. Many a parent has wondered if all this fuss is worth it just to go to the dentist or grab a bag of groceries! However, this fussing is an important step in the understanding of our physical separateness from others, and ultimately in further differentiating this understanding to our social connection to others.

Social development continues to grow with the contact of the parents and loved ones, and by one year of age, a child already has a pretty sophisticated means of socially manipulating its environment. For example, a little girl can bat her eyes and tilt her head in such a way as to say 'Am I the cutest thing you ever did see?' She in turn knows that this is likely to get Dad to pick her up and play 'goo-goo and ga-ga!' A little boy whose Dad had laughed the last time he demonstrated his new found skill of spitting into the bath tub, tries the technique out at the dinner table. He looks to his Dad for the expected response. He is puzzled when his Dad does not find it funny this time, and he shows his confusion with a furrowed brow. These examples illustrate the ability of the one-year-old to read expressions, understand some emotional content to those expressions and attempt to alter the social environment.

With the onset of verbal speech, the 1–2-year-old is establishing another tool to be used in their social repertoire. Non-verbal language, or the use of the face and body to communicate, are also developing during this time. This will be further addressed when we are discussing communication more fully.

Social impairment in PDD

The early stages of social contact, such as the infant establishing eye contact when feeding may or may not be altered in the child with PDD. Some parents report histories of early infancy that are no different than one would expect to hear from the parent of a typically developing child. These parents noted a diminishing of social contact, or a withdrawal from the child's social world. This loss of social progress, or detachment over time, can be indicative of PDD. With some children, the social impairment seen with PDD is more apparent early on. Parents may report that their child looked at the wall when they were breast fed, or just never seemed interested in being talked to. Some parents report stories of a child who was difficult to comfort or seemed generally fussy. These may be subtle differences and not of particular significance to parents until they are put into the total picture of altered development as the child grows.

Children with Pervasive Developmental Disorder may not demonstrate typical *separation anxiety*, as the impairment in social connection is such that to be separated does not necessarily cause them stress. Again, because of the wide range of developmental differences seen in the children with PDD, some children get quite connected to the parent and may have a particular difficulty in leaving them. These children often like routine and are comforted by knowing what to expect of the world around them. Change in that environment may be very distressing. This inability to adapt to new environments, or the strong desire to know what to expect, is often a struggle in the child with PDD. Having and displaying anxiety over separation, or change, in this light is not a stepping stone to normal social development, but rather a representation of the difference in the path of development.

Development of relationship

We have already talked a little about the early relationship to the primary caregiver. The power of this relationship has been well recognized for many years. As a matter of fact, this is felt to be such an important relationship that often when the child does not develop along the paths of normal development, the mother and/or father is the person blamed. It was not too long ago that 'the refrigerator mother' was supposed to be the cause of Pervasive Developmental Disorder. It is now universally thought that this is certainly not the case. The early social development of a child with PDD is not about what the parent did but about who the child is! When the naturally occurring process of social development is in its early stages and is not progressing as expected, it is due to some difference in the functioning of the brain itself. It is not fully understood exactly what the specific causative factors are, but by knowing that it is generally an instinctive ability of humans to develop socially, it is clear that this is likely due to something in our programming. And, when that programming goes askew, appropriate social development does not occur.

Peer relationships also start to develop very early on in the life of the child. Early relationships may possibly be siblings and observation of a one and a half-year-old playing with the toes of a new baby sister while cooing in her face, portrays this. Between two and three years children generally like to be with other kids but will play beside them rather than with them. This is called *parallel play*. Side by side, Allison and Joe play with their building blocks. They non-verbally define individual play zones and proceed to do their own thing. Joe will occasionally check on what Allison is doing and may imitate her constructed tower, or he may even invade her space to get hold of some more red blocks. This will be met with some resistance and soon the mother is on the scene discussing sharing and playing nicely. New skills are learned and Joe goes back to his space, and builds his red tower. Allison then invades his space for some yellow blocks and, although he is initially hesitant to try out the sharing thing, Joe does allow her to take the blocks for her house. The children are very aware of each other, but essentially play on their own. They will interact in the play setting and begin to work on the skill of cooperative play.

Cooperative, or reciprocal play, is when the children actually interact with each other in the play schemes. As they approach three years of age, children are more interested in playing together rather than beside each other. Allison and Joe may still play with building blocks, but as their interaction skills progress they will be seen building a town, with Allison working on the store while Joe builds the school. Soon they are discussing what else they want in their town and Joe helps Allison gather all the red blocks for her house.

Interactive play skills continue to develop and are really very sophisticated by four years of age. By kindergarten children know the social rules required to join a group at the lunch table and what is appropriate behavior to be socially accepted. For example, a five-year-old knows the voice and volume with which to announce his arrival in the library, quietly and politely, versus the voice volume he can use at the ball field, where he can be loud and jubilant. He knows that it would be inappropriate to jump onto another child or sit too closely to a friend at the library table, yet when greeting his friends at the ball field he squeezes onto the bench between two boys. Children continue to practice social techniques and progress with their peers in what is socially appropriate and acceptable. Though social skills are already very advanced in the school age, that is not to say that the process of socialization does not continue to grow throughout our lifetimes. Even in adulthood we practice our social skills. Many of us could cite examples of recent social 'faux pas' we ourselves have said or done. Looking at those settings helps us to refine our own social skills. Social training occurs over a lifetime.

Development of relationships in PDD

Connectedness to people around us develops along a predictable and observable path flavored by the child's personality characteristics and temperament. When we say that this process is predictable, that is not to say that children look the same socially. While Mary has no problem jumping into a circle of friends, Daniel may find it quite intimidating. Both children, however, are socially aware and 'normal'. Their individual personality characteristics are influencing their social interactions, but not necessarily causing them to be inappropriate. Without this innate connectedness and naturally developing social awareness over time, it is quite difficult for the child with PDD to fit in, or be indistinguishable from his or her peers in a social setting. Even among the high functioning children on the spectrum, their social interaction is often described as 'odd.' One parent commented that 'My kid doesn't seem to know how to be a kid.' She was referring to her child's awkward attempts at playing with other children, and a sense that, though she could not quite put her finger on it, his behaviors were different and a little bizarre. It is not uncommon for parents to state that their child socializes better with adults. Adults are more willing and able to modulate the interaction to better suit the child with PDD. The nature of the social developmental course is different in children with PDD, as they do not pick up on social cues spontaneously or have the ability to apply social skills in a flexible manner. Sean observed a daughter hugging her mother, who was a teacher, in the playground. Later when Sean saw the teacher in the corridor he ran to her and hugged her. Though he had not even met her before, he thought this was how to greet this woman, and he was confused when his classmates chuckled.

The child with PDD establishes a very concrete set of social rules over time and attempts to adhere to these rules in various social situations. This may be, in part, a reason that going to new places is difficult for a lot of these children. They are not comfortable enough with their social skills in unknown environments to know what to expect or what will be expected of them.

Having discussed the nature of the altered path of social development in the child with PDD, now let us acknowledge environmental influence. What we do to influence the child through our interactions in his/her environment can have a great impact on the ultimate social functioning of the child with PDD. This is particularly true of high functioning children and Asperger. If we leave them to their own skills, some will mature and learn skills on their own. However, it does remain likely that they will continue to have problem socializations. Social skills and the rules of our social world can be taught to a good degree but for children with PDD these rules need to be spelled out more clearly and broken down. In typical parenting we may prepare our children, in that when visiting Aunt Edna, we keep our hands folded and sit quietly on the couch. In this sort of situation we think ahead to let the children know what is expected of them. With children with PDD we need to think about this sort of prepping in all social situations. We cannot take for granted that the children will instinctively know how to act, or will be socially comfortable. This is particularly true if it is an unfamiliar environment where different demands are placed on the child.

By teaching the child what is appropriate socially and providing him/her with some tools to help them manage socially we may greatly influence the ultimate development of social skill. Looking back at the example of Peter in the playground, he lacked the understanding of personal space and wasn't able to initiate social interaction appropriately. Peter needs to acquire *the unspoken rules*, and to do so they need to be spoken and taught to him. For example, Peter can be taught not to get so close to other children when he wants their attention, but rather to say something. He can be taught appropriate verbal openers: 'Can I play that with you? I'm interested in trucks too!' He needs to have it reinforced not to fixate on stories and factual recitation, as that is very likely to turn off other children. When a child is thought to be 'odd' by peers, he/she is less likely to establish relationships that allow them the chance to practice and progress with social skills. Not only do they then have fewer opportunities to practice, but they may become more anxious about social interactions and decrease their desire and attempts to socialize.

The notion that social skills and understanding of the subtle nuances of a social setting is in part teachable, is evident when one looks at various cultures. For example, it is appropriate in some cultures to bow upon greeting, rather than shake hands. In some cultures it is not socially acceptable for women to show their faces in public, yet in United States culture women showing their faces in public has led to a multi-million dollar make-up industry.

As previously mentioned, the impairment in socialization is across a spectrum. The children at the milder end do not have finely tuned social skills and may be considered distant or odd, while children at the other end are completely disconnected from those around them. The less severely impaired children are more likely to be able to pick up on social rules and the cues that are taught to them.

Temperamental qualities come into play as well. The more out-going child with PDD may have a stronger interest in acquiring social skills than the shy individual, therefore, the rewards of working on social skills is built into the social interaction. The reward is the positive response from another child or enjoyment of the playtime with other kids. The child who is less interested in working on these skills may need to have another reward system, or means of encouragement, to work on these skills. They may need direct assistance with social cueing and guidance in the social setting until they can establish some comfort level with their own skills.

For the child who is more severely impaired socially, the acquisition of skills needs to be broken down into small components and taught step by step. For example, the first objective is to get the child consistently to look at people in the face. This then needs to progress to components of a social interaction. Conversation openers, verbal responses, appropriate distancing and all the other factors that are looked at when breaking down a social exchange need to be taught, piece by piece. This can be achieved by different techniques and working with qualified professionals who can direct the intervention and promote developmental progress.

Frequently asked questions

Why does my child prefer to play alone?

This is dependent on the degree of social impairment. For some children this may be because they are not connected enough to others to even be interested in seeking social interactions. For others, it may be that they do not have the social skills to initiate interaction and do not know quite how to go about it. The other thing that may play a role here is how other children have responded to them over time. Perhaps past attempts at socializing have caused other children to shy away from the child with PDD, giving that child fewer opportunities to establish and practice social skills. When self-esteem is bruised the child may come to prefer to play alone.

Can a child who likes to be hugged have PDD?

It is not true that all children with PDD are resistive to physical contact and comfort. Many children are affectionate while others are less so.

Can they have PDD if they had good eye contact as an infant and still look at me?

Yes. Some children do not show any symptoms of PDD until after their first birthday and up until that time demonstrate completely normal development. Others never had good eye contact and yet others have fleeting eye contact, meaning they will look at you and look away. Some children vary in their eye contact during the day, or day to day. One day they may seem more connected than on another.

How can this play out over time? How will they be when they are grown up?

This is the million dollar question for all parents. Let us start by saying that no parent can look at their three- or four-year-old and say they will go to college and marry the person of their dreams. We do not take on the job of parenting with a crystal ball, but in the family of the typically developing child, the parent does not have the fear that their child may not be able to live independently.

The optimum level of social functioning depends on how severely impaired the child is; effectiveness of interventions and social training; acquisition of language and communication skills, and level of intelligence. Most children with Asperger Syndrome, or the mildly impaired, have some persistence of social oddity but can live independently and have fulfilling jobs. These jobs are likely to entail skills that tap into their strengths such as space conceptualizing or the physical properties of things. Things that they choose to do tend to have a very specific focus, require concrete information, require repetition and/or are mechanical in nature. They may not demand a great deal of social interaction.

Children who are more severely impaired may have a very difficult time living independently as they do not achieve the necessary social and communicative skills to manage their lives. Managing money, tending to physical and medical needs, and even grocery shopping, are tasks of daily living that require adequate social skills.

CHAPTER 3

Communication

A powerful tool

Communication is our means of sharing information, ideas, thoughts, and feelings. The natural evolution of this process is perhaps taken for granted in the typically developing child. We tend to follow closely the development of speech and parents may know the exact number of words a child has at any given moment in time. However, the subtleties of total language and communication development, along with the production of sounds and words, is also progressing over time. This complicated process of communication involves not only the use of verbal language, but the in-depth understanding of the process as a give and take exchange. Non-verbal language is often as communicative as our words. Our body language, stance and positioning, intonation and volume, and facial expressions all contribute to the messages we convey.

Non-verbal communication

Some examples

PAINTING TIME

A group of kindergarten children gathered around the craft center. Mary takes her spot as far from Daniel as she can. She recalls the last time she painted with Daniel when he splattered red dots all over her creation. Her eyes meet his and she holds his gaze. 'I remember what you did, Daniel!' she communicates with her stare. She steps a bit farther down the table letting him know for sure that she 'was going to keep her distance.' Daniel's facial expression softens as he drops his head slightly. He briefly lifts just his eyes as if to say, 'I'm sorry. I didn't mean to do it.' Mary does not take his non-verbal apology well and busies herself setting up her supplies. 'I don't forgive you. Keep your distance!' she communicates clearly, without saying so much as one word.

This example illustrates how integrated communication is even before the school years. We perfect these techniques as we grow and establish powerful extensive non-verbal skills for use throughout our lives.

A BOARD MEETING

A group of people were sitting around a conference table. One shares an idea and then to reassure himself of the others' approval adds, 'You know what I mean?' He does not really intend to ask if the others understood the sentence he just spoke, he is asking for reassurance. He leans forward resting his arms on the table, and looks to get eye contact with one of the other parties present, further communicating, 'Would someone please agree with me?' The first person he connects with eye to eye, diverts her gaze and fiddles with the stirrer in her cup of coffee communicating, 'Don't want to touch that with a ten foot pole!' At the end of the table, a gentleman busies himself jotting on a piece of paper, communicating 'I'm busy with something else right now, can't address your question.' One person at the table is caught in his gaze and he slightly nods, indicating 'Come on, say something!' and the person responds with arms folded while leaning backwards in his chair. 'I see what you're saying.' His words hedge true agreement and his body language clearly confirms, 'I don't really agree with you!'

This very basic example of a communicative exchange demonstrates how much we communicate to each other daily with, and without, our words. Communication is a very sophisticated process and a very powerful tool in the functioning of the human being.

Children with Pervasive Developmental Disorder have an underlying impairment in the process of communication. An inability to use speech and language as an effective means of communicating as well as a lack of understanding the natural course of conversing, or the give and take exchange, pervades over the total developmental style and functioning of the child.

Communication early on

Typically, developing children understand the power of communicative exchange as a tool very early on. Young infants recognize that different cries are used to communicate different things. Sitting outside the door of a six-month-old's bedroom, one first hears some arousal from her nap. A few gurgle sounds and raspberries are heard. Shortly after she begins her whinny soft cry indicating, 'I'm awake now. Someone come get me!' The whine becomes louder communicating, 'Do you hear me?' The volume and tone are harsher, 'Hello, anybody home?' Until at last a full-blown wail ensues, 'I want out of here, NOW!' A child naturally comes to understand that he/she can manipulate their world by this wonderful game people play back and forth, called communication.

Following the establishment of early eye contact, facial expressiveness, vocalizations and early sounds, whining and crying, comes the progression of gesturing. By six months children will wave 'bye' and raise their arms when they want 'up'. They even start pointing for requests and/or choices. These early non-verbal means of getting their needs met sets the stage for later speech and language development. Early connection and this natural progress of conversing are the milestones that set a solid base for the entire communication process.

By one year of age, many children have a few words, with a *word defined as a sound that consistently means the same thing.* The sound 'ba' can be a word if it is consistently used to mean 'bottle'. By two to three years of age, children are putting words together and beginning to make short sentences. They share thoughts, wants, and concerns with their words, and their non-verbal skills. A toddler eagerly tells his mom that he saw a rabbit in the back yard. Even if his only true words are 'babbit' and 'out', he is able to share his story with enthusiastic intonation, excited facial expressions, and gestures for his entire story. And, most importantly, he is interested in sharing his experience.

There is a great deal of variation among typically developing children in the area of speech and language. This is mostly, however, in the area of *expressive language, or the use of words*. Some one-year-olds have as many as ten words, while some one and a half-year-olds are just starting to say some words consistently. Both of these sets of children may be considered to have normal speech if they are understanding language, communicating without words appropriately, and are interested in sharing wants, needs, likes and dislikes, and experiences with the people in their world.

Breaking the code

The process of learning language includes learning the *code, or grasping the symbolism of words*. This also entails being able to use language in and out of context. The code includes the letters, their sounds, and syntax and grammar. The rules of this code start to be learned by an infant and are nearly fully understood by five to six years of age. The understanding of symbols includes initially assigning meaning to concrete words, such as 'table', and progresses to actions, such as 'running'. Eventually these symbols are assigned to concepts, such as 'love'. While vocabulary is constantly being expanded upon and changed, even in adulthood, a vocabulary of several thousand words is already present in the preschooler.

The meaning of language in and out of context is the most sophisticated piece of learning in the language system. This includes understanding the meaning of a phrase by applying social and circumstantial information. To illustrate this point let's look at the words *hot dog*. There is a difference between a *hot dog*, a frankfurter in a roll; a '*hot dog*,' a kid doing flashy tricks on his skateboard; and a *hot dog*, a warm canine. One must apply more advanced understanding of the context the word is used in to accurately assign its meaning. Humor, irony, sarcasm, figurative speech, poetry, and other advanced uses of the human language, all rely heavily on the listeners ability to understand in context and to broaden their understanding to a brand new context.

A recap

With appropriate connectedness children learn early on that communication is a powerful means of having their needs met. This is accomplished by non-verbal and verbal means. The communication process advances to the production of gestures and then words. In its more advanced stages, language in linked to symbolism and imagination. The *code* is then more fully understood and we are able to advance to the point of de-contextualization, or the ability to apply various meanings to the same words, based on the context it is used in. As you can see, communication is quite a sophisticated process, which we often take for granted in the typically developing child.

The spectrum of impairment in communication seen with PDD

Not only is language development in children with Pervasive Developmental Disorder variable, but so too is the entire communication process. While some minimally affected children are relatively good communicators, others are more severely impaired in this area. There is always some degree of communication impairment in all children with PDD. The degree of severity of the impairment greatly influences the overall developmental growth and optimal functioning of the child.

Asperger Syndrome is characterized by superficially normal language development. This contributes to the high level of functioning of these children. Though they have words and can use words effectively, they are usually very concrete in their thinking and communicating. They often have difficulties with the use and interpretation of non-verbal cues. They are likely to have long-standing difficulties with the subtleties of communicating and understanding the emotional components of a communicative exchange. Children with AS and those on the high functioning end of the spectrum are often awkward in their attempts to initiate and maintain a normal conversation.

Pervasive Developmental Disorder is characterized by a wide variation of communicative functional levels. It is a fallacy that all children with PDD are non-communicative or that they do not want or desire to communicate effectively with their peers. Though this area is always affected to some degree, the presentation of the disorder changes greatly depending on the ultimate level of functioning in this area. Obviously, if a child has language and has a desire to relate to his/her peers to some extent, they will be more able to develop social and communication skills than the child who has little to no language and a lack of desire to socialize, or connect, to another child.

It is not uncommon for parents of Asperger and PDD children to have concerns about their child's hearing, because the child doesn't consistently respond to being called. It is usually not the hearing that is the cause of this lack of response, however, it is more due to the focus of their listening. Children with PDD may not even turn when their mother calls their name 17 times with various volumes and intonations. They will, however, cover their ears when the phone rings. They have what might be considered very selective hearing, or more accurately, very selective listening.

The child with Asperger Syndrome and other high functioning children with PDD may have good language skills but seem odd in their conversing, in that they are more likely to have committed learned words and phrases to memory. They have difficulty applying necessary flexibility and appropriate social rules to a given setting, or to a conversation. When their social skills and communication skills are challenged in a conversation with a typically developing child, the child with PDD may revert to sharing information that is rote and more comfortable to them. For example, they may appear to be reciting information about an area of interest, or repeat a favorite jingle, rather than appropriately respond to another child's question.

Compounding the problem of learning good communication skills is the fact that often children with PDD are viewed as odd by their peers so they are given less of an opportunity to practice communication and social skills. Children with PDD can be aware of the struggles they have and certainly can be aware that other children do not want to be with them some times. This makes them more uncertain of themselves and less likely to want to challenge and expand their skills. As for people who go to foreign places, they learn the language ahead of time only to discover that the culturally specific use of language changes the foreigner's ability to interpret or to carry on a conversation. For the child with PDD, perhaps it is as if he or she is a foreigner in their own land.

Children with autism, and the more severely impaired on the spectrum of PDD, have more severely impaired speech and language development. Some have no words, others have words but cannot use them appropriately. In these children, the impairment in the socialization process and the communication process are both so hindered that independent functioning in later years is unlikely.

As stated, children between the mild end of the PDD spectrum to those more severely impaired have many different presentations and qualities to their speech and communication techniques. The terminology for the type of communication disorder that children with PDD have is referred to as a *semantic pragmatic communication disorder.* The disorder is characterized by inaccuracies of *semantics*, (or the structuring of words into meaningful phrases), and poor *pragmatics*, (or the social aspect of the communication process).

Some definitions

Semantic disorder: The inaccurate structuring of words into meaningful phrases.

Pragmatic disorder: Lack of connection in the communication process. Inability to grasp the social component of conversing.

The core deficit in communication struggles for children with PDD, centers around semantics and pragmatics. How to put words together to make sense and how to connect that to the social circumstances they are in is exceedingly difficult for these children.

Echolalia: The repeating of part or all of a sentence. Described as 'ping pong' language, the same words go back and forth, but nothing meaningful is exchanged.

'Johnny, do you want an apple?' *'Wan an apple.'* 'You want an apple?' *'Wan an apple.'* When given the apple he puts it on the table. He was just repeating the words, not making a request.

Pronoun reversal: The inaccurate usage of pronouns.

'He likes meat balls.' The child meant 'I like meat balls.' *'Give it to him,'* instead of 'Give it to me.'

Reversal of meaning: What they say is not what they mean.

A child with AS is on the phone to his mother. *'Is mother here?'*

Recitation: Repetition of something that they heard.

'It's the real thing. Coke is. That's the way it should be!' Used in conversation and not intended to communicate anything in particular.

Associations and recitation: These are used rather than appropriate words.

A child seeking milk in her cereal always says, *'Does a body good!'* She is attempting to communicate something in particular but is using the wrong words.

A child who is familiar with computers says *'Click here'* at every stop sign on the road. (That is an icon often used to exit children's programs.) He is attempting to communicate that he wants to get out of the car.

Factual: Recitations rather than conversation.

When asked about what he did last night, a child recites the weather forecast, verbatim.

'Winds were out of the east at 40 miles per hour...' His vocalizations mimic that of the weather man.

Concrete thinking: Evident in their language.

After riding over a large bump the mother explains that there was a 'depression in the road,' the child with PDD asks, *'Why was the road sad?'*

Use of language out of context: The inappropriate changing of topic or flow of conversation.

Child in a conversation about sandcastles begins to talk randomly about Beluga the whale.

Inability to make appropriate openers: Not being able to initiate a conversation.

A child trying to play with other children runs up to them spontaneously and says, '*Party of four, your table is ready!*'

Unusual prosody: The pitch and cadence of speech.

Also, described as 'sing song' nature to their speech pattern. They may sound like they are singing or speaking another language.

Unusual tone or volume: Vocal quality is different without physiological cause. They may sound monotone.

Frequently asked questions

Why was my child slow to talk and then came out with full phrases?

Language development is not *delayed* but *different* in these children. The reason this pattern occurs is not clearly understood. Language is such a social act that problems in relating and difficulties with socialization are almost always coupled with impairments in the communication development of children with PDD.

Why does he echo me?

Echolalia is commonly seen and it is a part of the confusing picture of language development in children with PDD. Because they don't grasp the give and take process of communication, they are more likely to copy, or recite, than add onto an idea or expand on a thought.

How is it that he can recite an entire video and not say he wants juice instead of milk?

He does not understand the power of communication as a tool to meet his needs and wants. Children with PDD frequently do well with the rote aspects of language. They are good imitators and have highly developed memories, but only for some things.

Why does he pull me everywhere?

This is a more primitive way of getting some needs met. Usually children will do this for basic needs. If gestures and words are missing, then a physical prompt may be the only way for the child to communicate.

Does my child have normal hearing?

Generally, children with PDD have good hearing but lack good listening skills. They may be selective in what auditory stimuli they respond to. A child may not seem to notice you closing a door behind them, but the same child covers his ears when the blender is turned on. While hearing loss is not typically associated with PDD, if adequate hearing is in question, it is indicated to look into it further.

How will this play out over time?

Children with PDD, particularly those on the milder end of the spectrum, may develop good language skills. It is likely, however, that most will persist to have some degree of difficulty in understanding the subtleties of the human language and its abstract meanings. They will likely remain concrete in their thinking and conversing.

A final note

Language skills are crucial to the overall, optimum development of a child with PDD. It is critical to address this issue promptly and vigorously.

CHAPTER 4

Impairment in Play Style

The playroom is the classroom for the young child. It is in this classroom that we can learn a great deal about how a child is learning and developing. The way in which a child manipulates toys, explores his or her environment, sets up play schemes, and interacts with others in play, tell us not only how a child is learning, but also how they are assimilating and relating information from the world around them. It is in the playroom that children with Pervasive Developmental Disorder reveal yet another difference in their style of development.

CHELSEA

Locks of red curls bounce as Chelsea, a three-year-old, enters the play corner of the doctor's office. A kitchen set catches her interest as she checks out its cabinets and shelves. Finding some miniature pots, Chelsea sets about the task of making pretend soup. Small blocks are stirred in a pan as she asks her mother if she would like some soup as well. She pretends to wipe her hands on her apron as she's certain this is what one does when the soup is ready to be served. She has observed her mother do this many times. No soup bowls are to be found, so Chelsea makes do with a teacup and carefully pours the imaginary food into the cup. Carefully, balancing it to avoid any spills, Chelsea carries the tray to serve her mother, who tastes the invisible soup and compliments the chef. 'Would you like some crackers with that?' she asks her mother.

RANDY

Randy holds tight to the grasp of his mother's hand as he enters the doctor's office. Not one of his favorite places, Randy hovers behind his mother's leg as she signs them in. While waiting, Randy spots the knobs on the play kitchen set up in the corner. As he pulls his mother with him, he approaches the play area. Baskets of colorful building blocks, dolls, and other toys surround the inviting children's corner. Randy's mother picks out a dump truck and tries to engage Randy. 'Oh Randy, look what I found?' she entices. Randy seeks his own toy as he rummages through the large bucket. As Randy's mother returns to her seat, he begins to line up an assortment of Matchbox cars. He continues to add one after the other to form long rows. The rug directly under him is decorated with streets and a town designed to use with cars but Randy does not seem to notice, or show any interest in the cars driving through the pretend town. He remains content to align his cars.

The difference in these two children's play certainly illustrates the potential difference seen between the play style of a typically developing child and one with PDD. These examples are given for the purpose of clarifying the difference but it must be noted that the difference can be much more subtle. Again, each child has an individual presentation and may have a greater or lesser degree of impairment in this area.

Let us look more closely at these two examples to explain more fully the issue of a child's *play repertoire*, or a child's inclusion of skills and social understanding in their play. Chelsea recognized the connection of the pretend kitchen set to a real kitchen. She was able to apply her understanding and observations of her mother's role in the kitchen into her imaginary play scheme. This application of real life events into a child's play is a way for the child to practice what goes on in the real world around them. It affords them the opportunity to imitate appropriate social behavior and learn from the imitation of others' behaviors.

The ability to make a connection between the pretend and the authentic is observed early in a child's life. Young children will imitate combing hair, feeding a doll, or hugging a stuffed animal.

They indeed have the capacity to apply the use of imagination to set up a pretend world that mimics a real social world around them.

Now let us look at Randy's selected play. Firstly, the hesitation to step into new play environments is apparent for some children with PDD. Often the need to know what to expect or anticipate from a given situation may preclude them from becoming interested in toys in such an environment as the doctor's office. The knobs of the kitchen set were the first enticing item. Randy then proceeds to mechanically investigate the Matchbox cars. He spins the wheels and manipulates them for the purpose of examining their parts, but misses what they are, as a whole, an imitation of a real life automobile. He does not attempt to apply the cars to the rug-town streets, or demonstrate an understanding that these miniatures represent, or symbolize, something in his world. Randy misses any broader play scheme, while he physically explores, rather than applies an imagination to his repertoire. The lining up of items also is something commonly seen when watching a child with PDD play. Sequence and order seem to, in some way, give pleasure and are a predominant theme of much play for many of these children.

Spectrum of impairment

A child with Asperger Syndrome and those mildly affected on the spectrum of PDD may have very minimal impairment in this area. They may have the capacity to find the symbolism of toys and can apply that understanding to their play. They may demonstrate the use of imagination to apply their understanding of their real world to their pretend play. Often, their difference in social understanding can be revealed in play. While a typically developing child imitating his father mowing the lawn may interject visiting with a neighbor, the child with PDD fails to see any relevance to the exchange and is more interested in the mowing action. A child with PDD may not choose play schemes that are socially loaded to begin with as this just doesn't catch their fancy. Playing school, for example, with a group of dolls may not be desirable to a child with PDD. While they may play school, they may not apply a lot of social interacting and relating with the dolls. The child who can use a log as a rowboat, has to have a real oar, and no one is asked to join him in his boat.

As you can see in the higher functioning children with PDD, the impairment in play repertoire, or use of imagination in their play may be very subtle. As one moves along the spectrum, however, the impairment becomes more noticeable. Children more severely impaired may spend a great deal of time lining things up in rows. They may be content to spend a good deal of time moving one given part of a toy rather than applying it to any imaginative play. Play is observed to be very repetitive and in some cases to the point of restricting them from moving on to other toys or activities. In addition to this repetitive pattern of play, the child with PDD may have a repetitive pattern to what they choose to play with. Parents often report that their child is particularly taken with one toy, or category of toy. For example, trains have an incredible appeal to many of these children and we can only guess that this is related to the fact that they run in sequences. It is not uncommon for the child with PDD to be so interested in one area or topic, that they develop quite a particular knowledge in that area. For example, a child may know and be able to identify all the characters for the 'Thomas the Tank Engine' series, or know all the names of dinosaurs. This limited degree of interest is a prominent characteristic of the disorder. A depth of knowledge is not necessarily a bad thing but a problem arises when it is to the exclusion of other play, or restricts participation in more socially-loaded interactions.

With a greater degree of impairment and an even more limited repertoire of play, the child with PDD may be more physically driven. Play may be observed to be internally driven and of a physical nature; running around in circles and not seeming to notice play apparatus or toys, repetitively throwing toys over the back of the couch, and content to do this over and over again, or to be content to look up at a fan and hum. These all represent the most severely impaired along the spectrum. Their lack of connection to the world around them influences their development to the point where there is no appropriate play to represent a social world.

Certainly, the issue of whether a child will be able to play effectively with trucks when he is 20 is not the point. It is the greater picture of the basic understanding of the symbolism in things, and that the world is not a concrete setting but rather changes with varying social settings and varying environments. Flexibility in the application of our social rules and subtle connections are to be gained after accomplishing the classroom of childhood; the playroom.

Frequently asked questions

How does this play out over time?

No one has a crystal ball. The optimal functioning of any child with PDD very much depends on all areas of impairment, and they do all inter-relate. A child with a more severe social impairment may not work on communication skills to the extent of a child who is more socially adept. In turn, a child with more limited social skills is less likely to apply those to their play schemes, or expand on social learning through play.

Why does he always line things up in rows?

Sequencing and repetition are certainly a theme of play for many of these children. A sense of order seems to be comforting to them. And again, they may not see or be interested in the symbolism of toys.

Why does he always play with the same things?

Children with PDD do seem to stick to the same items over time. Some certainly expand on that theme, but many choose one item to the exclusion of a whole world. It is their comfort with sameness and discomfort with change that probably contributes to this.

Why does she become fascinated with just one aspect of the toy?

Physical manipulation of a toy is common among children with PDD. They focus on the movements of a toy, or the mechanical parts. They miss the bigger picture, so to speak.

CHAPTER 5

More Characteristics

Alteration in sensory perception

We are fortunate today to have adults who were diagnosed with autism as children and now are able to share their perception of sensory input. Because we cannot get inside of the head of a child with PDD to hear as they hear, feel as they feel, see what they see, this shared information has confirmed that children with this disorder have a different way of filtering sensory input and making sense of it. It is for this reason that some children will be particularly sensitive to sounds, lights, and touch. The same child who won't so much as look up when you ask if he wants more milk, three times at the dinner table, is the child who hears the fire siren four blocks away, or covers his ears when the radio is turned on. Perhaps, for one child the flashing on a computer game is just too irritating, while for another it is fascinating to watch the flashing lights. The alteration in sensory processing may cause one child to insist upon wearing long pants in the heat of winter and yet another child is not even able to tolerate the tags inside the back of his shirt collar. The inability to tolerate some touches is called *tactile defensiveness*. This can even carry over to textures of food that a child will not eat.

There is a great deal of variation from child to child with regard to what sensory stimulation is enjoyed, as well as what is intolerable. This altered process dramatically influences a child's reactions to the outside, stimulating world. As adults, we take for granted the ability to filter sensory information. When sitting across from a friend at the lunch table we are able to focus on the conversation. We will not be tremendously distracted by the noises of others in the cafeteria, or the slight flickering of the fluorescent lights overhead. Think of how difficult it would be to connect socially to our friend across the table from us if all the sensory input around us received equal processing value. It would be exceedingly difficult to carry on a conversation surrounded by echoing sounds and blinking lights. Perhaps, this is not unlike part of the struggle for the child with PDD.

How do we perceive?

This question has been the subject of scientific and philosophical debate for years. Much more complex than simply the reception of information through eyes, ears, or skin, it is also the interpretation of that information that comes into play. Memory, emotion, combinations of sensations are all involved. We can only begin to have a shared understanding of perception because we probably have similar ways of sensing our world. The antithesis is also true, however. It is clear that everyone does not have similar ways of interpreting sensations and understanding the world. Did Mozart hear music like others? Did Monet capture and interpret light like others? Does Michael Jordan perceive the distance from his hand to the basket like others?

While we can't fully understand just how others perceive, we can be certain that there is variability among the general population. Mozart may have *seen music* in his mind's eye, visually composing as if painting a picture. Perhaps this gave him an ability to conceptualize the total composition rather than the individual details. How did Einstein perceive and understand mathematics? He had a capacity for looking beyond numbers to see the more expansive patterns of numbers. He did not merely look beyond what others had studied; he studied things differently. These examples help us to understand that, while most of us probably have a degree of shared perceptions, there is variability in those perceptions, and some people view the world in a very different light. While physical input may be the same, the intellectual perception, or interpretation, is different. It is very possible that this is the core difference in sensory processing for many individuals with PDD.

Without a means of filtering out stimuli, or weeding out the sights and sounds that are not useful at a given time, a child with PDD may feel overloaded by input. Compare this concept to a birthday party at the arcade. After being bumped into by a hundred small children, hearing the sirens and wails of the video-games, and watching a group of children run about in utter chaos, one feels as if they might burst from sensory overload. Perhaps a child with PDD has a lower, or different, threshold level. The child with PDD who has a lower, or different, threshold level for stimulation may be living with just such an arcade in his head.

We need a heightened awareness of this sensory difference in children with PDD. When they are 'losing I,' it is not enough to say 'He's got to get control of himself.' We need to look closely at what in his/her environment could be causing an overload. Attempting to better understand what it is that they may be experiencing can help one intervene in the most effective manner. It might be as simple as escorting a child out of a crowded room, or teaching a child to turn down the volume on the stereo system and dimming the lights.

Alteration in motor function

Coordination and control

Many children with PDD have a delay in the acquisition of motor skills. They may be somewhat slower than their peers to walk or run, and in many cases when they do start to walk they seem unsteady in their gait. Many parents describe their children as 'clumsy.' 'They don't seem to know where their body is going,' said one father. This delay has been looked at from various points of view and different explanations are given by professionals in the field of developmental pediatrics.

Even simple movements have a complicated brain process behind them. The fine tuning of walking, for example, is under the control of multiple brain motor control centers. These centers control the gradation of movement, balance, muscle tone, and coordination.

There are also neurologic centers that are responsible for evaluating the purpose of walking, which entails the social implication of walking. This concept is illustrated when watching boys 'strut' down the street, as compared to cheer-leaders who 'bounce' as they walk. Our gait, therefore, can be thought of as part of our non-verbal communication. Because the master control mechanism in PDD is frequently tuned differently, it is common to see a combination of awkward movements. To make matters more confusing, the affects are not uniform. Some highly complex motor tasks may be very well developed, while simple tasks are poorly developed. A child who is able to climb proficiently, walks up on his toes in a bizarre pattern.

A second explanation for the alteration in motor skills seen in PDD children is because they are not fully connected to their surroundings. Due to this they have poorer *motor planning*, or understanding of one's body in space. They are not fully sensing themselves in the space around them as they move about.

A third explanation is, because the basis of PDD lies in the neurochemical or neurostructural functioning of the brain, it is very likely that the brain functions responsible for motor control are also affected. Again, as we learn more about the complicated central control system, we may have a better understanding of the more specific alteration in brain functioning in children with PDD.

Physical mannerism

Children on the spectrum of PDD are often noted to have unusual movements, or *mannerisms*. These mannerisms are also referred to as *stereotypic* movements, as they tend to be repetitive in nature and can involve the whole body or isolated parts. A child will rock or sway rhythmically, another will flap his hands. Facial grimacing and strange vocalizations often go along with the physical movements, or can be seen or heard separately.

Unusual movements and mannerisms can occur spontaneously, or they may be triggered by excitement, boredom, or anxiety. The predictable movements are frequently habit-based, that is they are done repeatedly out of habit. Many people have mannerisms due to habit. Thumbsucking is a socially appropriate stereotyped movement seen in infants and small children. Adults may twirl a strand of hair or stroke at a beard. Individuals with PDD commonly have stereotypic movements that are not appropriate, or considered socially acceptable at a given time or in a given circumstance. Hand flapping, spinning, and head rocking are behaviors often seen in children with PDD that set them apart from their peers.

Children have these mannerisms for a variety of reasons. People are innately calmed, or soothed by rhythmic movements. Sucking, one of our very primitive reflexes, is very much a rhythmic action. Infants are calmed by rocking and swaying motions. This leads us to the notion that it is likely to be for the same reason that children with PDD do this. Furthermore, the fact that many children with PDD are not as socially aware of what is socially acceptable among their peers or have not fully learned what is an appropriate social reaction, may lead them to respond in this more primitive nature. One mother shared that when watching a soccer game her son would flap his hands so much that he actually scared the other supporters of his team. It finally struck her that this was simply his response to the excitement around him. He was not able to pick up on how the other children were acting in this situation and he was internally driven to express himself in this way. It was, however, distressing to him that the other children were shying away from him, so he and his mother worked together on learning the appropriate response for this situation. His mother actually scripted a response for him to follow when he felt excited, and though it still appeared somewhat stilted in its performance, the boy's new found way of yelling 'Go! Go! Yea team!' was received much better by his peers.

Physical mannerisms are a cause of great concern to many parents as they are an outward sign of the internal difference in the child. Parents often respond to these bizarre looking movements with fear and anxiety. In stepping back from the situation and trying to take a more objective view, a parent may be able to better define what is the trigger for such behavior and come up with an effective plan to help the child be more socially appropriate.

Unusual strengths and skills

The development of specific areas of interest or advanced skills, beyond the expected level of competency for a child that age, is another baffling component of the disorder of PDD. This is most commonly seen in children with Asperger Syndrome, and it is a diagnostic criteria of the disorder. It can also be seen in other children on the spectrum of PDD. The 'not fully understood' brain function in these children, again causes an unusual presentation of development of some advanced cognitive skill.

Early reading, or *hyperlexia*, is often a skill children with PDD possess. This initially presents as early identification of letters and quick memorization of the manner in which a book is read to them. Some children are reading well, before they even enter school. The level of oral reading skill often exceeds the comprehension level and when the child is asked more socially-loaded questions related to the content of the reading, the child with PDD has difficulty coming up with answers. We spoke to a little girl with Asperger Syndrome, *Amy*, who is five years old and has read the entire series of *American Girl* stories. These books are at about the third grade reading level and explore the lives of girls growing up in the different eras of American culture. Though Amy was able to tell in great detail the content of the books, she showed no emotional connection to what she had read. When asked how she felt about the girls, or for the girls in the various moments of strife and triumph, Amy was unable to answer and reverted back to reciting various excerpts that had been of interest to her. Amy repetitively reads the books now and enjoys them lined up in the series on her shelves. Though she has not fully understood the content of the stories, the fact that she can read is an incredible strength for her and other children who develop this skill. Because books tend to be so socially and emotionally loaded, they are great tools to use to expand a child's social understanding and emotional response. Stories have the capacity to tap into an area of deficit for the child with PDD and expand on skills.

In addition to hyperlexia, the skills of concrete learning of concrete things also applies to shapes and *spatial relations*. It is for this reason that high functioning children with PDD will know when their mother has taken a different path to the grocery store and will be able to direct their father to a park he has not been to before. Exceptional spatial concepts can also be illustrated by adeptness for puzzles. It is often reported that a child can do puzzles, which are way beyond the expected age skill level. Because the children have a propensity for these tasks, they tend to like them.

Any preference of play that a child has can then be used and expanded upon to promote growth in areas of weakness. These areas of strength are just that, areas of strength. With the proper education and guidance, a child can use them to expand on their less well-developed areas of communication, and socialization.

CHAPTER 6

The Evaluation Process

Where to start

Perhaps the hardest step in the process of having a child evaluated is the *first one: identifying that you need to.* Many parents have shared similar stories of their sense that something wasn't 'quite right' with their child, and yet were unable to actually put their finger on exactly what it was. Often, due to the limited amount of time that pediatricians and family doctors see a young child in the office setting, the problems associated with PDD are not revealed. 'Red flags' may go up for some doctors when parents share concerns regarding eye contact, lack of speech and communication efforts, but more subtle differences seen in children more mildly affected on the spectrum of PDD may not be deemed significant. Peculiarities in play style, singular interests and difficulties with sensory input are just some of the characteristics that may not be highlighted to the physician. Physicians and professionals working with children are becoming more familiar with the changes in diagnostic criteria and terminology in the concept of autism as a spectrum. However, inconsistency and lack of current thinking in the field remain among many health and developmental professionals. Parent concern then often becomes the driving force behind further developmental assessment.

Another scenario may be the case. Physicians may become concerned about a lack or difference in speech development, variation in motor skill development, or difficulties with tantrums or unusual behavior. They may not be specifically thinking about the diagnosis of PDD, but they may be concerned that there is a difference in this child's style of development and seek the guidance of a professional with more expertise in the area. Parents may not yet be concerned, however, that Johnny doesn't point or Sally is a little clumsy. A pediatrician may be quite concerned about a child's lack of connectedness and refer with the suspicion of PDD.

In all of these scenarios, ones in which the parents have concerns and ones in which a physician or another party initiated referral, the assessment process is a trying and difficult time for parents.

Finding an evaluator

Referral to an evaluator can be done via a variety of options. First, discuss with your primary doctor your concerns and ascertain his or her recommendations on how to proceed. In such a case, medical referral can be made to a developmental pediatrician, neurologist, psychologist, or child psychiatrist. Developmental evaluations may be accomplished by non-medical professionals as well. Public health offices can direct a parent to a means of evaluation for the young child. Local school districts will be able to direct parents in regard to developmental and educational evaluation for the school age child. Often evaluations are accomplished by a team of professionals. These teams include combinations of the many professionals including: medical professionals, educational specialists and therapists, and psychologists.

Specialists and roles

Developmental pediatrician: A pediatrician with additional specialized training in fellowship beyond his/her pediatric training.

Child psychiatrist: A medical doctor with specialization in psychiatric and developmental diagnosis.

Pediatric neurologist: A doctor with specialization in neurologic conditions.

Developmental nurse: A nurse with further training and experience in child development.

Speech pathologist: A master's prepared professional with expertise in speech and language.

Special educator: A teacher trained to work with children with special needs.

Social worker: An individual with a master's degree in social work.

Physical therapist: An individual trained to work with motor needs of children.

Occupational therapist: An individual trained in working with use of hands and functional skills of daily living.

Psychologist: An individual trained in clinical psychology, developmental psychology, school psychology, or related degree.

Because parents going to the evaluation may not yet know the specific diagnostic concerns they are facing, it can be hard to hand-pick who would best serve them. Parents should rely on the professionals they trust to guide them.

Regardless of who the evaluation is completed by, parents should feel comfortable with how the evaluation went and have confidence in the professionals who are in the position of diagnosing and determining their child's needs. We would encourage parents to seek out further information through second opinions, reading material and from other parents, if they feel the need.

What to expect from the evaluation

Depending on the background of the examiner, or team, the process of the evaluation will vary. The tools used, or the developmental tests and materials worked from, will vary. There are also some tools designed more specifically for the area of autism that may be useful. An important point to note, however, is that the nature of PDD is such that the diagnosis is made by the appreciation of the qualitative differences in the areas of communication and especially social relatedness. This is accomplished often through the level of experience of the examiner. In a good evaluation, the examiners are able to get a thorough and complete medical, developmental and genetic history; observe play, socialization, and direct interaction with the examiner; and conduct some cognitive testing to get a sense of the child's level of intelligence. It is often difficult to achieve the latter of these, as children with PDD do not always reveal their true cognitive, or problem solving, abilities in a test format. Many of these children 'underscore' and are actually quite bright. Some actually have exceptional intelligence, albeit while seeing the world in a very different way. Thus, parents should cautiously respond to scores from standardized IQ testing.

The developmental history, or story about how the child has progressed, is very important as it is often the nature of developmental progress that illuminates the difference in the style of development in the child with PDD. A child having language and then losing it, or the child having the ability to recite a commercial he has seen, but not being able to ask for juice, are peculiarities in the course of development that may not be revealed by standardized testing, but rather by developmental anecdote.

Furthermore, a child's degree of connectedness is something that is more observable than testable. It is difficult to quantify, or objectively give a score or value to the presentation of this area of impairment. The examiners rely on their understanding of normal development, knowledge of the characteristics of PDD and overall experience to recognize the disorder. The length of the evaluation process then is not always directly related to an accurate evaluation. It is difficult for some parents to accept that such a diagnosis can be made after a professional has only spent limited time with the child. Again, it is the appreciation for the areas of impairment and level of expertise with this population that influences the accuracy of the diagnosis.

Physical examination and medical work-up

Any time one is looking at development, the child's physical and health status needs to be taken into account. A medical history and a brief physical examination should be performed. The examination is usually unremarkable, in that children with PDD tend not to have physical differences. There are a few other diagnoses that may need to be ruled out, however, and these may be taken note of on physical examination. An examiner will look for *dysmorphisms,* or *unusual differences in physical appearance.* Facial features, hands and fingers, as well as other body parts, may point to a genetic syndrome or condition. On physical examination, children with PDD may have a large head size, although this does not necessarily point to a structural difference in the brain itself.

Medical testing

'Can't you run a blood test to know for sure?' was the plea of one mother in need of medical confirmation to accept the diagnosis. Unfortunately, the answer to that question is 'no'. Currently, no medical testing can confirm the diagnosis of PDD, but some testing may be indicated and ordered by your physician.

Blood work requires the drawing of blood from the vein of the child. It is then analyzed in the laboratory. For example, there is a genetic condition known as fragile X (addressed later), which can be detected by *chromosomal testing.* This looks at the genetic 'blue prints' of the child and, while this cannot be altered by any medical intervention, it may assist with diagnosis and is information that may be important in terms of family planning for other family members. Blood work and urine tests may also be looked at for *metabolic conditions.* These are uncommon in children with PDD.

An MRI, or magnetic resonance imaging, is a means of looking at the brain structure. It entails placing the child on a stretcher, requiring restraint and/or sedation because he has to lie absolutely still, and wheeling him into a large cylinder. Pictures of cross sections of the brain are taken and they are read by specialists in radiology. This is a costly test that also has a low yield, meaning that it is rare to see a difference in the brain structure of a child with PDD. Remember again that the difference in the brain may be on a chemical level, not structural. Lastly, nothing can be done to change the established structure of the brain. It is for all these reasons that MRIs may not be done on children with PDD for the purpose of diagnosis. Parents have a hard time understanding this, perhaps because they are seeking some tangible, clinical indicator of the disorder.

EEG: Another test that may be done on a child with PDD is an EEG, or electroencephalogram. This test entails placing electrodes with a gel-like substance on the surface of the child's head. There are many electrodes to place and, though it is helpful to have the child awake, but sleepy for the procedure, it is difficult to get a child to let examiners accomplish this. The purpose of this test is to look at the electrical wave patterns of the brain. It is designed to look for seizure patterns. This test may be ordered on a child with PDD if there is any indication that a child is having spells that may be actual seizures. It is helpful to do the study because there are medications available for seizures and treating them effectively is important to a child's health and development.

New and more powerful ways of understanding the electrical activity of the brain may offer us important information about PDD. Such procedures include a *magnetoencephalography, MEG,* and a *continuous EEG* recording. For example, the developmental regression that occurs in many children with PDD has been thought possibly to be related to a seizure condition (Lewine *et al.* 1999). Research is still in the early stages but deserves following.

Can anything else look like PDD?

Laundau Kleffner syndrome is a seizure disorder that can be mistaken for PDD and autism. Children lose their ability to speak due to changes in the electrical patterns of the brain. It generally occurs in older preschool children and is uncommon. It is diagnosed by completion of an EEG. Some medical treatments have proven helpful to children with Laundau Kleffner syndrome (Lewine *et al.* 1999).

Fragile X syndrome, mentioned earlier, is a chromosomal syndrome consisting of a constellation of physical differences including; large head, cupped ears, altered hairline, large body size, poor learning capacity with high rates of mental retardation, poor language development and social disconnection. This can overlap PDD.

Can we avoid labeling?

No parent wants a child to carry a label that he or she thinks will stigmatize their child throughout the school years and perhaps beyond. The label should be used to support the parent and child in establishing that there is a biological difference in this child, which is causing the differences in development. In other words, poor parenting, or just being a 'bad kid' are not the cause of his difficulties. The label should be used to help specify the areas that need to be addressed vigorously. The label should be used to help elevate the child to a better place, not to diminish him. The label should help get the child what he needs. It would be untrue if we said that all professionals, educators and people in a child's world are going to fully accept the child with an open mind and not carry preconceived notions of what it is to be autistic, or have PDD. Parents are forced to take on the role of educating others as to what the diagnosis means, and more specifically, what it means to their special child: what strengths and weaknesses they bring to the playground, back yard and classroom. Issues that go along with the concept of labeling a child are changing as society is changing. Acceptance of differences in schools and communities is certainly improving over time, and, with every child who has PDD who grows and makes a contribution to the world, the misconceptions will improve.

CHAPTER 7

What Can Be Done?

Medical Perspective

Treatment and intervention is decided upon and initiated after the diagnosis has been made. Much can be done for children with PDD. Having a clear understanding of the struggles that the individual child faces is a huge first step. We are then able to most effectively work with him or her.

The next two chapters will look at the medical and educational perspectives of just what is being done for children with PDD. We touch on some key components and intervention modalities, but this is certainly not intended to be all inclusive of all methods of testing or intervening. Nor is it all inclusive of the multiple opinions of professionals in the field.

There is currently no medical cure for Pervasive Developmental Disorder. There is no pill or treatment that attacks the underlying difficulties. Research in the field of psycho-pharmacology has led to a boom in the treatment of many adult psychiatric and emotional disorders. This new information about medication options will very likely in the future be applied to the pediatric population. Also, more is being researched and understood about the chemical and physiological processes of the brain every day. It is likely that significant advances in biologic interventions will take place in the near future.

Though the disorder as a whole cannot currently be treated with medications, many of the complicating factors or co-existing conditions can be managed effectively with medications. As mentioned in the previous chapter, several of the secondary issues may respond well to medication management. It is felt that even though we cannot directly treat the underlying cause, medications can be useful in children with PDD in an attempt to peel away the layers of various difficulties. In this *onion peel* approach to medication management, we look to eliminate some of the most significant struggles and issues, in the hopes of optimizing strengths and promoting learning and social development. For example, if a child is so motor driven that he is unable to sit and focus for any productive period of time, it may be helpful to take the edge off the hyperactivity. Perhaps then, educators, parents and therapists can have a more powerful influence on that child. In the same way, if a child gets stuck on a thought or a repetitive behavior, it may be helpful to treat the obsession so that the child is freed up to work on functional skills.

Another issue that can be treated with medication is mood stabilization. Often children with PDD swing through periods of highs and lows. They may experience periods of being more *turned on* and periods of being more *tuned out*. They may have periods of escalated anxiety alternating with calmer times. These mood fluctuations can be a considerable source of distress and here specific medications may prove to be helpful.

When thinking about starting any child on a medication, several things need to be taken into account. Every medication intervention carries with it inherent risks of side-effects and the pros and cons of any medication for a given child need to be looked at carefully by the prescribing doctor and parents. It is necessary for the parents to have a good handle on the child's behavior prior to the medication trial so they will be able to record and evaluate the child's response to it. They need to be able to accurately communicate changes, side-effects, and/or benefits to the physician. The doctor may prescribe the medication, but the parent is the one who is living with the child. Parents are truly the experts in regard to their child's behaviors. It certainly takes a qualified medical professional to manage a new medication for a child with PDD, and it is for this reason that often a child psychiatrist, child neurologist, or developmental pediatrician is consulted in these matters. Sometimes, family doctors and pediatricians are comfortable prescribing more commonly used drugs, but in other cases they may refer a family for further professional input.

Before starting any medication

Before starting any medication, it must be clear exactly what is being treated. For example, it must be determined whether *Julie*'s circling the living room repeatedly is related to *hyperactivity* or an expression of *anxiety*, in order to most specifically treat the problem. This can be achieved by looking closely at a behavior over time. Taking notes and keeping a journal are very useful tools to help define and isolate behaviors. It is important to look at what had been happening before the behavior, what might have triggered the behavior, or what might be *precipitating factors*. Keeping a journal can help a parent sort this out. If *Elizabeth* consistently rocks excessively before getting on the school bus and before going to her grandmother's house it may be more a product of anxiety than hyperactivity. But if she randomly runs in the yard at a neighbor's, that may be more a component of hyperactivity.

Before starting medication, it also must be determined if the behavior being targeted is indeed impairing the child to any significant degree. Is the hyperactivity preventing the child from being able to sit and focus? Is the anxiety blocking his or her ability to work on social skills? It is also reasonable to think about how the child is co-existing in a family, when deciding if a medication trial is appropriate. If the child is so obsessive that the family can't get through a decent meal because the child has to repeatedly touch her fork and then her knife, it can wreak havoc on family life. That's not to say the physician should medicate a child because the family can't get through a meal. Rather it makes the point that the overall influence that the child's peculiarities are having on the family and their life in general, should be taken into account.

At what point to start medication is determined by the physician and the parents. Parents should feel comfortable with the decision and have confidence in the expertise of their doctor. Parents will need to be in contact with the doctor to let him/her know of the child's response and to make any adjustments that are indicated by the physician. Medication should not be stopped abruptly without notifying the physician, as some medications have to be weaned, or reduced gradually.

If the child is old enough and able to understand, it is important that the child is part of the decision making process. They need to know why a medication is going to be started and what they will need to tell their parents about if they experience side-effects. They may be fearful of a medication if they do not know what to expect from it. They need to know that the medication is supposed to help them in a certain area and why changing that would be helpful to them.

All trials of medication are just that, trials. If a medication is started and it does not provide the desired response, or if side-effects emerge, it can be stopped. Finding the right medication, in the right amount, for the right child, can be a process of trial and error. Sometimes, a particular medication may not work well for a very young child but when tried at an older age it is effective. Therefore, parents should not feel that if a medication does not work at one point they should never try that medication, or others, again.

It is important to know what side-effects to look for with any given drug. Journal keeping can be helpful in gathering the information into meaningful terms. For example, if meals are recorded, it is easy to see if appetite has waned during a medication trial. If not written down, it may be difficult to recall small changes over time.

Common medications

This review is intended to be only a brief look at some more commonly used medications. It is by no means all inclusive of the many medications currently available. Additionally, if one of these medications is used for a child, the parent should get further specific information regarding the drug from his or her doctor and/or pharmacist.

Attention/impulse control

Psychostimulant drugs

The most common treatment of attention/impulse control symptoms are stimulant drugs, which improve focus and sustained attention. *Methylphenidate (Ritalin), Dextroamphetamine (Dexedrine)*

Desired effect: Decrease in activity, increase in attentiveness.

Method of administration: Given by mouth. *Ritalin* and *Dexedrine* work quickly and have to be given in doses over the course of a day. They often require administration at school or other settings outside of the home. Both also come as long-acting preparations.

Side-effects: Loss of appetite, nausea, difficulty sleeping, rebound (worsened behaviors as the drug is wearing off).

Hyperactivity

Clonodine (catapres)

Desired effect: Decreased hyperactivity, decreased aimless excessive energy.

Method of administration: Commonly given in a patch form so that the medication is absorbed over time. The patch only has to be put on every few days and therefore, this drug doesn't require frequent administration. *Clonodine* also can be given in pill form by mouth.

Side-effects: Local irritation at the site of the patch. Some children do not like the feel of the patch on their skin. Significant sedation can occur. Lowering of blood pressure may occur. This medication may not be stopped abruptly.

Obsessive/Compulsive Disorder

Antidepressants

Selective Serotonin Reuptake Inhibitors (SSRIs) are the drugs of choice for this disorder, along with different types of antidepressants.

Fluoxitine hydrochloride (Prozac), Sertraline (Zoloft), fluvoxamine maleate (Luvox), Clomipramine (Anafranil)

Desired effect: Decrease in obsessive compulsive tendencies and treatment of depression.

Method of administration: Given in pill form by mouth.

Side-effects: Increased anxiety, nausea, vomiting, headaches, worsened hyperactive behavior, loss of appetite and sleep difficulties.

Mood stabilization

If there is a strong family history of bipolar disorder (manic depressive disorder) or depression, a doctor may be more inclined to think that a child may be struggling with problems of mood. In such cases, and others that seem to manifest fluctuations in moods, mood stabilization, especially *anticonvulsants*, may be used. Originally designed for the treatment of seizure activity, these drugs have also been helpful in treating PDD children. They have been around for a long time and they have been used with children for a long time, so they are deemed reasonably safe in the pediatric population.

Anticonvulsants

Carbamazepine(Tegretol), Valproate (Depakene,Depakote)

Method of administration: Given in pill form by mouth.

Desired effect: Calm the child, prevent and treat mood swings, especially over-excitement.

These drugs require to be at a certain level in the blood to be effective. Therefore, blood may need to be drawn on occasion to make sure that it is in the right quantity in the child's blood system. If the level is too low the drug may not be working. If the level is too high the child may have unwanted effects such as staggered gait and clumsy walking.

Side-effects: Vomiting, abdominal pain, unsteadiness.

Other medications

Other medications are sometimes used to treat anxiety, self-abusive behaviors, aggression and thought disorders. More specific drug choices for an individual child should be addressed with a medical doctor.

Some comments on secretin

Secretin is a hormone that recently gained some interest as a potential treatment for PDD and autism. The naturally occurring hormone was given a very favorable slant by media coverage in the United States. Anecdotal reports of children with autism whose symptoms decreased after receiving secretin were the subject of several television reports. These reports stimulated many parents to ask about the treatment and seek administration of it for their children. While it is quite reasonable to have a positive initial response to such information, it is important to slow down and examine the information more closely.

Secretin is essentially a substance secreted by the pancreas that assists in the process of neutralizing stomach acids. It is used currently in the medical community during diagnostic testing of the intestinal tract. Some information publicized through television media showed children with PDD given secretin were observed to have improved communication and social skills. The findings were quite promising but were limited. Further research is warranted and will probably be forthcoming. Most pediatricians who are specialists in development would still take a very cautious approach to secretin administration until the questions of its safety and effectiveness are more fully and adequately answered.

Many important scientific discoveries stem from clinical observations and random findings. We can be encouraged by any positive responses by the children, but we must look at treatments with an empirical eye. Controlled research provides the accurate answers we seek and it is to this we must look. Parents and professionals in the field of developmental pediatrics are very committed to supporting such research. It is an optimistic future.

CHAPTER 8

What Can Be Done?

Educational Perspective

This chapter will look at a few of the modalities of teaching that are predominantly used today. It will give some guidelines for determining what therapist and/or program will meet an individual child's needs. Hopefully, this will help you answer for yourselves; 'Where do we go from here?'

The logical next step following the diagnosis is seeking appropriate interventions and education for a child with PDD. There are many good programs and many dedicated people working with these children. They are committed to making a difference and they surely do. However, this remains a confusing and sometimes overwhelming time for parents as they are in the throws of just beginning to understand what the diagnosis means, and trying to accept the implications that it has on their child and their family. In the midst of this, they are challenged with the task of learning about the multitude of modalities of teaching children with PDD, selecting the best option for their child, and finding therapists and/or a program. This is quite a project and takes a great deal of effort, but there are people who can support parents through the process.

Getting started

There truly is something for everyone out there. An alphabet soup of educational terms and an array of theorists result in a diverse selection of educational opportunities for children with PDD. While evaluators can help guide families by clearly defining the child's areas of need, parents are truly at the helm of the decision-making process in regards to implementation of servicing. The first step is for the parent to get informed as to what the various modalities entail and what is available in your area. They may find it helpful to obtain the support of professionals in your region or area to assist in this process. Offices of early intervention, or school departments of special education may be places to seek out such support.

It is not uncommon for a parent to read of a very specific teaching strategy for children with PDD, only to find that they do not have access to a program or therapist with training in this particular method. Often, 'variations on a theme' so to speak are available and with good research, parents are usually able to find the appropriate intervention available to their child. Parents should meet with therapists, go to see programs in action and discuss the child's individual needs. They should determine how a given therapist or program would address these needs. Parents have shared that they generally ended up with a 'gut feeling' about what was the right thing to do. It can often be the trained specialist who 'clicks' with a given child and has multiple options to implement in the educational process, that has the greatest impact on that child. While strategies and modalities are certainly important in providing a framework for intervention, we encourage parents not to feel that they have to take only one way to education. It can be hard to know from the outset what methods will be most effective for a child. Again, parents should be informed as to what has worked for other children with PDD and what is available to them. They are then in a better position to make a decision.

This brings up another important point. What if a parent does not find anything in their area that they think supports an appropriate education plan for their child? The parent now is in the position of advocating for implementation of such a program, or training. We advise that if such is the situation, a parent should obtain valid research and published information on the modality that they are trying to have implemented, and present it to the persons in their area who are in control of programming issues. This may be a person in an early intervention office or someone at the school district. Professionals in the field of child development are often open to furthering their own educational background, and/or trying out new strategies or methods. It might just be an issue of setting up the appropriate means of educating the people who would be working with the child with PDD. Due to expansion of diagnostic terminology in this field and the increasing number of children being diagnosed, it has been our experience that therapists and teachers are very interested in expanding their skills in this area.

Another issue of concern in determining the best intervention options for a child with PDD has to do with intensity of servicing. Due to the great need for intensive socialization and communication intervention, these children often benefit from special schools and programs This is true even for children as young as two-and-a-half to three years. It has been felt in the past that young children benefit from working in the familiar environment of their home. This can be a good place to start, certainly if a child needs some time to become familiar with therapists, to be able to comfortably work with them. It has to be noted, however, that it is most beneficial to immerse the child with PDD into the more social context of a special classroom, or integrated program, to optimize opportunities to work on socialization and communication. It is heart-wrenching for some to send a toddler off to a school, but we need to emphasize that the one thing that we are sure of for children with Pervasive Developmental Disorder is that the earlier and more intensively we directly work on the areas of impairment, the more likely it is that the child will have significant adaptation to the developmental disorder. To optimize school age placement with minimal support, much work needs to be accomplished for all children with PDD, regardless of where they fall along the spectrum. Decisions regarding where and what interventions will be implemented also depend on the age at which the child is diagnosed. It may be reasonable to start a very young child with intervention in the home setting to acclimatize both the child and the parents to the educational process. While in the case of the child first diagnosed at more than three years of age, it is almost always indicated to place the child into a center-based program.

How to proceed

First, parents need to familiarize themselves with the roles of the different therapists, and the various educational modalities and intervention methods. We will look at some of the most common modalities. When reviewing your child's options specifically, it will be important to seek further reference material for the given methods and interventions. It is important to meet with potential therapists, and visit programs using various methods and see exactly what they do day-to-day. Even if a program says it follows a certain method, there is so much variability in the way that programs are implementing these techniques, that the actual programs are very different. For instance, two programs that use *applied behavioral analysis* (ABA) may actually look very different in practice. Also, two speech therapists may have very different styles and/or teaching strategies within the same framework of speech and language therapy.

Roles of related services

A diverse group of educators and therapists work with children with PDD. Each area of expertise focuses on given areas, but all take into account the multifaceted nature of children. For example, one cannot work exclusively on the area of speech and language development without taking into account the child's play and learning style. Additionally, within a group of therapists of a particular orientation, there is variability in methods of practice, techniques used, levels of experience and personality characteristics. All these factors influence the effectiveness of the interventions employed.

Speech therapy is a cornerstone of intervention for most children with PDD due to their needs in the area of speech and language. The role of the speech therapist in this population is important not only in helping the child with the production of words and understanding of language, but more importantly, in helping the child understand the power and process of communication. Speech therapists are trained professionals with an advanced degree in speech and language pathology. They use a variety of methods to facilitate the development of language and conversational skills.

Special educators are teachers trained to work with children who have special needs. Levels of preparation vary from associate degrees to those with graduate degrees. The approaches and techniques vary from one therapist to another depending on their training and experiences. Special educators can be very important to the child with PDD in their effort to promote socialization skills, establish more productive and useful play skills, and to fill in the gaps in scattered learning skills. They also help with the expansion of communication skills.

Physical therapists focus on the gross motor area, or area of motor control of the whole body. They are versed in the expected body movements of children and work to establish appropriate movement and physical skill. Because some children with PDD have differences in their body movement and coordination, physical therapists may be helpful.

Occupational therapists work with fine motor, or hand usage, as well as an array of self-help skills. Children with PDD often have difficulty controlling their fingers and hands to do effective writing, cutting, use of eating utensils, and such. Occupational therapists also work to develop appropriate activities of daily living skills, such as dressing. Some occupational therapists have particular interest and expertise with children with PDD and focus on the child's response to sensory input. They may be able to help with the child's response or aversion to certain feelings on their skin, called *tactile defensiveness*. The term *sensory integration* means different things to different people, but in this context, it is used to mean the efforts that a therapist will put into helping the child receive sensory input, tolerate it and make sense of it.

Social work and psychology are related services that play an important role in the child with PDD's intervention plan. These specialists work with the child to help with behaviors and social skills. Some design behavior modification plans to eliminate unwanted behaviors or foster desired behaviors. Social workers and psychologists can also help with social skill training. Parents often benefit from the guidance and support of these professionals, and, particularly for older children with PDD, it is important that they have a professional to help them work through feelings of insecurity, alienation, and possibly depression.

Methods of educational intervention

Applied behavioral analysis (ABA)

ABA has become increasingly popular in the recent past, though the grassroots of behavior modification, its broader term, have been around for decades. What perhaps is new, is the intensity and amount of time that people are using this technique with young children with PDD. This approach came from an advocate for intensive application of ABA among the PDD population, O. Ivar Lovaas (Maurice, Green and Luce 1996). Some programs call their methods 'Lovaas' but are actually more of a variation on the theme. Many other educators, psychologists and developmentalists have designed training programs on the basis of behavior modification, which are effective and not necessarily as intensive as that of the Lovaas school of thought.

Another term is often interchanged with ABA and that is *discrete trial training*. This interchange is incorrect, as discrete trial training is only a part of ABA and is a technique used for specific teaching situations. Discrete trial training is one-on-one instruction, in which the teacher prompts a desired response (done in a variety of ways), the child gives the response and gets a reward, or reinforcer. A reward can simply be praise or a small token. If the child does not give the desired behavior, some programs give no response, some give negative reinforcement (not popular among most parents) and some correct the response.

Discrete trials are used to accomplish specific simple tasks, such as consistently looking at someone in the face. 'Look at me!' has become the mantra of many parents. When more complicated skills need to be mastered, they are broken down into smaller, simpler pieces and trained one by one in this format. Eventually, these simple components are strung together for completion of the more complicated task.

The amount of time spent in discrete trial is dependent on the given program. Some therapists and/or programs spend short periods of 5–10 minutes every hour, while others spend ½–1 hour, five times a day. Some do discrete trials in a separate confined space while others are found prompting a response and giving a reward in the middle of 'circle time'. No two programs apply this method in the same fashion.

Every child who receives intervention through the modality of ABA does not necessarily need discrete trial training. The higher functioning children with PDD may have already mastered many simple tasks taught in the discrete trial setting and intervention time may be more wisely spent in social group settings. Again, ABA programs implement the use of discrete trial training and methods of behaviorism in different ways.

Regardless of all the controversial issues surrounding its usage, and inconsistent application of the method, ABA can be a strong strategy for teaching skills and changing behaviors. It is for this reason that parents should familiarize themselves with the basics of ABA, whether they choose it as the primary modality for their child or not. It can be a useful component to any individual plan, and for some children, modified use in a more natural setting can be very beneficial. It might not take hours sitting across from a trained teacher for some children with PDD to 'look at me' but implementing the reward system component of ABA in the classroom may be a useful tool. Conversely, a more severely involved child with no eye contact may require multiple discrete trials before they will meet your eyes. Any, and all, approaches need to be individualized to the given child's specific needs.

Applied behavioral analysis begins with *observation and analysis* of a behavior, or skill, over time. The task at hand is then broken down into smaller parts and those parts are then taught singularly with each success being *rewarded*. These small pieces are then strung together until the child has acquired the new skill or task. A cornerstone to this method of teaching is the ongoing *recording and evaluation* of the responses. Constant modifications in the methods need to be applied. While parents can learn this technique and do it on their own, it is helpful to have the guidance and experience of someone familiar with the techniques in order for its application to be most effective.

An issue that must be addressed when working in the framework of ABA is *generalization*. Generalization is the ability to take what is learned in one setting and apply it consistently in other situations. Children with PDD have a very difficult time with this, as they are often concrete learners and the carry-over of skills is hard for them in different settings. A child sitting across the table from a teacher in a discrete trial can say, 'Hello, my name is Sally.' This isn't useful in the bigger scheme of things if the child is not able to do it anywhere else. Efforts to foster generalization have increased as awareness of its importance has come to the forefront. Establishing functional use of skills has got to be a key focus of any intervention strategy. Consistency of training among many people in the child's world, as well as applying the basic techniques in everyday living, are important means of promoting generalization.

Special education provided in play setting

In this method of special education, teaching is accomplished through play. Various teaching strategies are used with toys and play schemes to expand on the child's view of the world and to develop skills. Toys are generally representative of the real world and, therefore, are inherently useful tools in expanding a child's repertoire. Play is not random in therapy sessions but rather it is directed by the skilled therapist to foster development of the specific skills associated with a child's social world. The effective therapist focuses specifically on the child's individual existing repertoire and expands to meet their greater needs.

When watching some special education methods in action, parents may think that all the therapist is actually doing is playing with the child. They may be left thinking that this is not an effective modality because it doesn't look much different to how they have already been playing. This method really does require a great deal of expertise, however, to be done correctly and to yield the desired learning and play skill development. When left to their own devices, most children with PDD will be quite limited in their style of play and area of interest. It does not benefit them to be stuck in limited play schemes. They need to be directed and led to expand on their play. Teaching needs to be in a systematic and thoughtful manner under the guidance of an experienced therapist. In effective play therapy sessions the environment is structured to eliminate distractions and encourage attraction to desired items. The teacher continuously engages the child. The teacher, or child, initiates the play and the teacher then promotes elaboration and expansion of the play schemes. Evaluation of progress is essential and feedback results in modifications in programming.

A key point is that the actual therapist is as important as the modality. Good therapists know how to get the desired response from a child and they can work wonders. As discussed in previous chapters, play is a very important pathway in understanding the social world that we live in. Play in this respect is often limited in even the higher functioning children with PDD. Play skills need to be worked on for every child with PDD in a supported, structured way.

Social adaptation intervention

An effective means of interacting and intervening with children with PDD has been found to be by *social adaptation*. Taking the view of the primary struggle being social difficulties, these approaches focus specifically on fostering growth through helping the child learn a means to adapt and socially connect. Various programs utilize this concept. A sample of one such program is *The treatment and education of autistic and related communication handicapped children (TEACCH)* (Mesibov 1994). Techniques employed by this program are being successfully implemented in many other programs and utilized by therapists.

TEACCH (TREATMENT AND EDUCATION OF AUTISTIC AND RELATED
COMMUNICATION HANDICAPPED CHILDREN)

TEACCH is a program used exclusively in North Carolina for the early intervention of children with PDD. Programs outside North Carolina are incorporating TEACCH components. Educational environments are structured to encourage skill development in specific areas of impairment. Individual assessment and programming occur with a focus on communication and socialization training. Children are observed at length to establish a baseline of skills. Communication skills, both verbal and non-verbal, are then built upon. PDD is viewed as a *multidimensional variation in development* and teaching methods are designed to cross that multi-dimension. Generalization is a priority, and parents play a large role in fostering it by keeping abreast of what is being implemented in the classroom and bringing those strategies to the home setting.

Structure and routine are cornerstones of this method. Also, learning is fostered with many visual cues. Children with PDD are not usually auditory learners. In other words, it is hard for them to learn from what is spoken to them. In the TEACCH modality, this issue is specifically addressed by visual supports and the expanding of existing skills by visual means.

Emotion and relationship based intervention

Yet another way to approach intervention for the child with PDD is to focus on the development of appropriate emotional response and relationship building. These programs prioritize the need to relate in 'real-life' settings, and specific guidance is given on how to achieve that. A sample of one such program was designed by *Greenspan* (Greenspan and Wieder 1998). Stanley Greenspan, a psychiatrist from George Washington University, looks to relationship-based intervention rather than behavioral approaches. His approach is developmental because he sees PDD as a *multisystem neurologic disorder* (Greenspan and Wieder, p.8).

The Greenspan intervention method requires the manipulation of the child's environment to cultivate interrelation, engagement and sensory regulation. A primary emphasis of this model is on attaining more appropriate emotional responses.

Listening and learning are not felt to be the way to reach children with PDD but rather developing real-life interactions, repeatedly, with the necessary guidance. Language is addressed first on the non-verbal level with promotion of gesturing. Affect is cued; in other words, children are trained how to emotionally respond. Work is done in small, manageable steps. Family involvement is also a cornerstone to this approach.

Communication augmentation

Some programs emphasize the visual learning style of the child with PDD. Viewing the core deficit in PDD as that of an inability to understand the social communication process, these programs specifically implement visual strategies. One program that encompasses this idea with theory from the behavioral camp was designed by Andrew Bondy (Frost and Bondy 1994).

The Picture Exchange Communication System (PECS) was developed to work specifically with children who have communication disorders that are due to a lack of social understanding and awareness. Behavioral techniques, such as giving a concrete reward, are combined with the use of pictures to foster communication. Children are initially prompted to make requests or initiate an exchange, and they do so with a tangible picture. The process is rewarded and success is then built upon. While this is not an extremely difficult procedure, it does require training in order to be most effectively implemented. The key concept of using visuals, and focusing on the need to develop social interaction, are components that can be applied to any teaching strategy for children with PDD.

Implementing therapy

Now that you are a little familiar with the modalities being offered to children with PDD today, let's look at how one actually has the intervention implemented. We spoke briefly before about the issue of having interventions provided in the home, or in a more specialized school setting. If a parent has chosen to have the child receive servicing in the home environment, they are then in the position of finding the person, or people, to do that. Therapists and teachers who go into children's homes can either work independently, or work for a program, but visit the homes to provide servicing. In either case, a parent needs to select such a provider.

Selecting individual intervention specialists

Many therapists and special educators will meet with parents prior to being chosen as a provider. Others are unable to due to money and time constraints. If one cannot meet in person, perhaps they may be available by telephone interview. Some parents are intimidated by this process, but it is certainly their right to know something about a person prior to that person coming into their home to work with their child. Therapists often welcome an opportunity to address questions and issues ahead of time and will find most who call to be conscientious parents.

After having familiarized yourself with the major methods described above, ask the therapist or teacher what method he or she employs and why he or she uses that specific one. If she names a specific method, ask in what way she implements it. For example, if she uses ABA, does she do discrete trials or apply behavior modification in a play setting? Establish the reasoning behind use of a technique. It is important to know how many years of experience the provider has and the extent of direct experience she has with children with PDD. Is he or she familiar with the new diagnostic terminology?

The purpose of the questioning is to gather information and to then make a decision. If someone is new to the field, or isn't familiar with the term 'Asperger Syndrome', one may not want to automatically disqualify him/her. She may just exude the energy and enthusiasm, or share one's philosophy to the extent that your gut (led by your head) tells you that this person can help the child.

Practical issues are a factor as well. When a therapist is available and how flexible she can be, may be an issue for a parent. Does this schedule work in the real everyday workings of a family?

How she sees the parent's role and how she intends to include the parent in intervention and decision-making is an important question. Most therapists have frequent, ongoing communication with the parents but, particularly if the parents work outside of the home and are unable to be at therapy sessions, this has to be firmly established ahead of time. Ideas to support good exchange are essential; a daily log for both therapist and parent to write in, a weekly phone conference, or even a monthly consultative meeting to discuss where the child is, gains they have made, needs that persist, and to evaluate the overall intervention plan and response.

Finally, if more than one therapist is going to be involved in a child's plan, they will need to coordinate therapies. Parents need to get the sense that they will be team players and that the therapist is not a solo act.

Selecting a program

Many parents decide that their child would benefit most from the more intensive environment of a center-based program, or specialized school. After becoming familiar with the various general approaches, it is important for a parent to get out to see the programs in action. Seeing is believing, or, more correctly, seeing is understanding. A parent is then able to make an informed decision as to what program would be good for the child. Most programs will give prospective parents a tour, review pertinent issues and address questions. Often parents can observe therapy sessions. Viewing the techniques, settings and hands-on components demonstrates a lot to the informed viewer. Schools are generally receptive to parents, and if they aren't at this stage, perhaps that's an important piece of information in itself.

The first thing to address is a program's overall philosophy and intervention approach. What methods are used and who implements them? What sorts of therapists, teachers and specialists will be working with the child? What are their qualifications, experience and expertise? How much experience do they have in working with PDD and what sort of success have they noted with these children? *Look at the actual structure and schedule of the day.* How long is the day and what amount of time will the child be in individual sessions? How much time will he/she be in group activity? Is all the time spent in structured activity, or is there free time?

One parent shared with me that her child attended a program for four hours a day, only to find out that she was out of the classroom for three hours of it for individual therapy. The mother's main interest in this program was the social interaction afforded in a small group setting, however, the actual structure of the day prohibited the child from seeing much of her peers. They modified the program so the child received the private therapy sessions at her home in the afternoons and was able to be more a part of the group setting during her time at the school.

Some practical things come into play when choosing a program. What is the class size and the staff-to-child ratio? How much one-on-one time will your child have? What sorts of special needs do other participants have? One may not want a child with PDD in a setting in which none of the participants have verbal language or any communication skills, for example. It is perfectly reasonable to ask specifically how the program *promotes social interaction.* Establish what is done in more specific scenarios. For instance, if the child likes to spin when excited, how would the staff members deal with this? Or, a child talks incessantly about trains, how will the therapist alter that? How do they manage tantrums?

Be clear on the role of the parent as viewed by the school. How do parents fit into the scheme of things? What is the means and frequency of communication with parents? What is available for parent education and support?

Evaluation of progress is key to being able to make the necessary changes to an intervention plan. If a therapy technique is not working, it needs to be looked at, analyzed and revised. All programs should have a format for data keeping and evaluation. Evaluation should be planned and not just be sporadic. It is not good enough to just 'sort of see where things are going.' Ask the program providers directly how they plan to review the child's gains, assess his or her ongoing needs, and address those needs or make modifications over time.

Uniqueness of intervention and programming

After having reviewed these different educational modalities, and there are many more educational philosophies not addressed here, let us get back to the point at hand. There are many therapists and programs. Each utilizes different methods; teachers and therapists contribute their own unique gifts, and many incorporate a combination of therapy methods to optimize the child's development. Therefore, the punch line is not so much what modality a therapist or program espouses to use, but rather what they have to offer the individual child. You have probably ascertained that we, the authors, do not exclusively support any one modality. It has been our experience that *different methods work for different children* and combinations of strategies can be very beneficial. A consideration also has to be what a family can realistically employ day in and day out. Whatever method professionals, or program families go with, they need to be truly committed to participating in its success.

Some key points

Regardless of the specific method chosen

1. Intervention plans need to specifically address communication and socialization skills.

2. Programming needs to be individualized and structured.

3. Professionals working with children with PDD should have appropriate background and experience.

4. The issue of generalization needs to be concretely addressed.

5. The program must record and review data over time. The evaluation of this information is then used to modify interventions as needed.

6. Parents need to be active participants involved in planning, implementing, and evaluating the child's programming.

7. The program should include a concrete means of regular communication and collaboration among teachers and therapists. Additionally, a formulated means of communication with parents.

8. All professionals working with the child need to have a good understanding of the diagnosis of PDD and how the individual child presents with the disorder.

9. Health department and/or school district safety requirements must be met.

Children with PDD in the school age years

It is not uncommon for children on the mild end of the spectrum of PDD not to be diagnosed until they are school age. Also, children who were diagnosed with PDD at younger ages are being integrated into the typical classroom setting. The needs of many children with PDD are best served in a typical classroom, but almost always these children need additional support. The characteristics of PDD are unique in the classroom setting and can easily be misunderstood. The child's inability to respond or participate may be misunderstood as defiance. Situations lead to the child being considered manipulative or having a behavior problem. The impairments in communication, socialization and restricted activity are part of a developmental disorder. All who work with the child with PDD should have a clear understanding of this.

Learning problems may emerge in school age children with PDD because they may have very strong skills in one area but may be totally lacking in another. The child who is doing 10th grade algebra in 3rd grade can have the reading comprehension of a first grader. Special supports should be designed for these children and they need to be very individualized. Special educators and subject tutors can lessen the gaps.

Another issue to be addressed in regard to the child with PDD in the classroom has to do with their difficulties with rigidity and inflexibility. This can be helped markedly by keeping the classroom structured and predictable. The child with PDD should be prepared ahead of time for changes and transitions. The use of a timer to let him know when there are just a few minutes left to an activity can be a simple way to alleviate troubles involved in moving from one task to the other. Also, a sequence of events presented in pictures can be used as a tool to help a child transition. They can be prompted, prior to a change in activity, to point or hand a picture to the teacher, a communication that they understand something else is going to happen.

For children with PDD, rigidity carries over to a fixation on concrete rules. These children can take rules very literally and will have a hard time following inconsistent use of rules. If they can't talk in line in the hallway, they may not understand why kids are talking in line in gym class. Rules need to be spelled out succinctly and followed as best as possible. Helping the child understand the flexibility in some rules can be achieved by training the concept. This is achieved by pointing out any time when they are flexible in a day by saying, 'That was very *flexible* of you when you did XYZ.' They then establish a more concrete understanding of the word and concept of *flexible*. When you later ask them to be flexible, they are able to follow the concept. This strategy can be applied to other concepts as well, such as: patience, understanding, attentiveness and cooperation.

Struggles with language can be managed in the classroom with the assistance of a speech therapist. Specific plans to assist the child with PDD in communicating his/her needs and wants, should be a major focus of intervention in the classroom, as it was in the earlier years. Language used with the child should be concise and clear. A furrowing of the brow from across the classroom may not be enough to get Alex back in his chair. Again, utilization of schedules and pictorial representations of language can be very helpful tools.

The special interests of children with PDD can be used to advantage, by implementing them into the child's lessons. If a child loves trains, stickers with trains on them can be used as a manipulative in working through math problems. Special interests can also be used as rewards. For example, when Sam can sit and do his maths for 10 minutes, he can then play with his train on the rug.

Problems with fine motor skills, or the child's ability to coordinate the use of his hands, may make it hard for children with PDD to work efficiently and in a timely fashion when handwriting is involved. The child shouldn't be pressured by time constraints whenever possible and accommodation for the additional time requirements should be taken into account. Occupational therapists can assist specifically in this area. It might be a reasonable consideration as a child gets older, to minimize the problem and stress of fine motor difficulties, by letting the child use a keyboard. When writing by hand is inhibiting the ability to get one's thoughts and information expressed, then perhaps it is appropriate to take that issue out of the equation of struggles.

Early reading skills are sometimes an area of strength for children with PDD. Though they can often read well mechanically, their comprehension may be behind. For this reason, they seem to have advanced reading abilities, while in fact they actually need remediation. Getting the content of what has been read, and picking up on emotional components of what they have read, may need to be more directly taught. There are so many wonderful books available to children, with a content that can foster better social understanding and provide a situation for the teacher to discuss social circumstances. This provides an avenue for the teacher to expand on the child's social understanding. Early reading can be capitalized on, but may need to be expanded upon by specialized help.

Children with PDD are not immune to the impact of others. As a matter of fact, older children with Asperger Syndrome have taught us that the reverse can be true. They are acutely aware of their differences and make a great deal of effort to be socially accepted. This is a hard task for many children. They may feel lonely and isolated, and this can lead to low self-esteem. They have to conscientiously work on issues that their peers pick up instinctively. This is a constant challenge for them. Attention needs to be paid to this issue and teachers, parents, and all who work with children with PDD, need to help build up, rather than break down these children. Positive reinforcement and praise goes a lot further than discipline and denigration. If symptoms of emotional problems arise, they should be addressed promptly with the assistance of professionals.

The child's development is not just about his or her special needs. Like for all children, parents should be involved in school activities. This indicates an interest in the child's world. Friendships can be fostered by getting children together or encouraging the child with PDD to join groups that share his/her interests. It can be hard for some children with PDD to play one-on-one initially, so it may be helpful to set up play dates by going to a museum or some other activity that incorporates social interaction but is not totally reliant on it. Praise social successes.

Additional tips

Communication assistance

Various communication tools that don't involve speech have been tried for children who have significant difficulties with language. Communication boards, or picture boards, are used to promote communicative exchange while not requiring the child to speak. Usually the boards have pictures of desired objects or actions and the child communicates by getting the picture off the board. There are some very elaborate computer communication boards available today. However, before incurring the expense of these, know what it is that you are buying. Look to people familiar with this assistive device technology for further advisement.

A lot can be done more simply. One therapist shared with me the type of board she finds useful. She begins by taking photographs of things the child likes. She initially keeps them in the 8 x10 size and the child actually takes the whole picture under certain prompts or questions. When the child demonstrates a good understanding of what the pictures represent, the therapist shrinks the picture to a smaller size. She continues to do this until they are small and can go on a Velcro board. The child continues to actually pick the picture off the board to communicate. Eventually, this progresses to pointing at the picture on the board. In this whole process, verbal and non-verbal language reinforces the visual.

Use of computers

Computers are powerful tools to children with PDD. For one thing, many children with PDD respond well to the concrete nature of a computer's functions. What you exactly tell a computer to do, it does. There is no need for much language interpretation with a computer. Children with PDD may have capabilities on the computer and these can be used to expand into other areas. It is not helpful to the child with PDD to sit down to do something rote and repetitive on the keyboard while tuning out the world around them. The use of the computer needs to be supervised to be beneficial. There are programs available of children's stories which are interactive and will promote interaction and expansion on social understanding. There are also programs designed specifically for special needs children that focus on language and communication. Communication skills training, language, activities of daily living, and many other topics are addressed by the multitudes of specialized interactive programs currently available. There are many specifically geared toward the development of conversational abilities and social understanding, not strictly language acquisition.

One final word

Education is a lifelong process and while we have a good deal to teach our children with PDD, we have a good deal to learn from them as well.

CHAPTER 9

Additional Options

Alternative therapies

Alternative therapies are essentially treatments that are somewhat outside of mainstream, or may not have been adequately studied for their effects or side-effects. Parents and professionals have tried a wide variety of treatments and interventions that were found to be helpful to a child, or a group of children. What works well for one, however, may do nothing for another. Parents have always searched for the one thing that will make a difference to their child. This is a good thing as parents are a powerful driving force behind the research work that is being done currently. A problem can arise, however, when information is shared on something that worked for one individual child and is then applied to all children without adequate study.

Testimonials, or the accounts of singular cases, can be helpful in a parent's attempts to share with others what has worked for their child, however, these should be viewed with some caution. A certain treatment may work for one but this does not mean that it is necessarily good for every child to try, or that it might not be harmful to a different child. The intention of this chapter is not to discourage parents from trying natural treatments or from sharing non-conventional treatments with others if they so desire. It is our hope that parents will be informed on how to better evaluate treatments, the validity of their use, and be able to identify potentially harmful treatments.

'Natural'

Be aware that just because a substance is deemed *natural* it does not mean that it is automatically *harmless*. Let us remember that some very strong drugs were derived from perfectly natural plants. Digoxin, a heart medication, comes from a foxglove plant for instance. Taken by the wrong person, it could have potentially serious deleterious effects. One can look at hormones as natural substances, but be reminded that they have some very powerful effects in the body. Think of insulin, the hormone responsible for controlling blood sugar levels. If it were given to a child with normal blood sugar levels it could be very harmful, if not lethal. Some naturally occurring substances need to be at a particular level in the body. Health food stores are very much in vogue these days for curing an array of ailments. People tend to be moving toward what they perceive to be more natural and harmless substances. This is not necessarily untrue, but one needs to be an *informed* consumer. So how does one become an informed consumer in the light of the contradictory evidence that is out there regarding just about everything?

Looking at treatments

First consider the testing and regulation of a given product. Most non-drug products are not regulated under the guidelines of the Federal Drug Administration (FDA). The FDA has very strict policies for the testing and administration of medications, and rightly so. It does not, however, have control over vitamin and mineral treatments, or even some of the more recent hormonal compounds. This means that there is no oversight, and no consistency among brands, regarding scientific testing of a substance. These substances often lack the testing that rationally and impartially questions product usefulness and safety.

Does this product have possible side-effects? What is appropriate dosing? How is it prepared in a compound for administration and what is it combined with to make it have a stable shelf life? Recently, a compound felt to stimulate memory had to be pulled off the shelf because it was prepared in an alcohol compound and under age children were taking it for the alcohol component, not to do better in their social studies exams. All this does not mean that one should never take a vitamin. It is just intended to encourage a parent to put up an antenna and find out as much as possible about something that their child is going to ingest, before making the decision to give it to them.

When looking at nonconventional treatments, there are options other than vitamins, minerals and hormones. Diet management has claimed to be of importance to some children. Therapies such as holding therapy, or dance and movement therapy, don't pose any physical harm and may help some children. Each of these, though they will not overtly cause harm, needs to be looked at objectively, as time spent nonproductively is valuable time lost. There is a tremendous maze of claims for helpful or curative approaches to PDD. However, claims that are not well studied and open to impartial review must always be looked at carefully. When in doubt, a parent is wise to call a medical center or a trusted medical professional to help with the overwhelming preponderance of information on multiple alternative therapies.

The quest for information
The NET

In this day and age we would be remiss if we didn't address the Internet and the volume of information literally at the finger tips of parents and professionals. There is something for everyone on the net and *surfing* it can prove to be beneficial, and overwhelming. The need to weed out what is valid and what is useless can be an arduous process. It can be worthwhile for those seeking to tap into resources and to connect with other parents and professionals outwith their area. Parents need to remember that the World Wide Web is a place of ultimate democracy. Anyone can put up any kind of information they wish. Well-meaning people and those out for material gain may publish approaches or information that is misleading, misguided, or inappropriate. When you see information, be certain that the source is reliable. The source should have some tie to a university, medical school, government agency, or well-established and respected private program. Look at claims and treatments closely. Is there data to support the claim? Has valid research been accomplished?

Support groups

Support groups can be very helpful to parents. There is nothing like working through problems with someone who has been there. Inherent in these groups, however, is the natural desire to compile children into the same expectations. Parents of children with PDD need to be particularly aware of the uniqueness of their children and use such groups which support and embrace those differences. Support groups can be cathartic, help parents make connections to other families, give a forum for concerns, and be a place for advocacy to begin.

CHAPTER 10

Up Close and Personal

Parents share their stories

The inspiration for this book project was spawned from the desire to address some of the issues parents face when going through the process of understanding their individual child's developmental style and differences. In talking with parents, it became strikingly apparent that many go through similar struggles and have similar experiences. It is positive for parents to know that their child is not alone in his or her challenges, nor is the parent.

These interviews touched us not so much by their content, though the stories themselves are moving, but rather by the strength and fortitude of the families. Love really can and does move mountains, as it has for these children.

Please note that the names of the children and the parents have been changed to protect confidentiality. While much of the interview contents are verbatim from the parents, some have been abridged and/or modified in an attempt to be more concise and understandable. The main ideas are those of the parents. The children discussed on the next several pages fall on varying points of the continuum of PDD. The children and their parents share many issues in common.

A special thank you to those who shared so openly. It is their desire, as it is ours, that other parents will learn and be comforted by what they have to say. Here are their stories.

About Lynn

Lynn is a little girl we met a few years ago. Over these few years she has made wonderful progress and is such a happy child. Like others, though she struggles with social difficulties, her uniqueness is a special gift. Lynn's mother, Cynthia, is yet another example of a parent's love put into action! This is their story.

'Such a happy baby!'

As an infant, Lynn was such a happy baby. A delightful child! She smiled and laughed, and she slept! I loved that, sleep. I have an older child and he didn't sleep so I loved that! She was a doll. We moved up here when she was about 13 months, and she had walked by her first birthday, she had a few words and was putting a few words together. At that point I was more concerned about getting my almost 3-year-old into nursery school. Then I had more time with Lynn, but by 20 months of age, I was beginning to get concerned. Her language had stopped. I didn't understand why she could sit and look at a video forever and why she wasn't interested in books. She didn't want to be read to. She would only let some people hold her and she wouldn't call me 'Mommy.' She really liked her Dad, and called him by name. They were very close. And, she liked her brother and called him by name. But she wouldn't call me by name. Looking back on it now, I think that I was just an extension of her.

'Then tantrums, as if you were sticking pins in her'

She didn't really lose her language and she could use words to get her needs met, but it didn't progress. She got stuck in time. And then she started to tantrum. Then came big tantrums. I tried to make her talk, thinking that if I don't get it for her she'll have to use words. 'Tell me this?' or 'Tell me you want juice?' She would just lose it totally. Throw herself on the floor. It would escalate as if you were sticking pins in her. Of course, I was concerned about her so I went to my pediatrician. I was a 'crazy woman' and was told to stop reading medical books. I would say to the doctor, 'Why is she doing this or that? There's something wrong, there's something wrong.' And he said, 'Stop comparing her to other children. She's a typical second child. Her brother is very talkative and she can't get a word in edgewise. Look how happy she is playing with her toy.'

Again, when I think back, she played with only one toy and it had to be a certain way. After talking to the doctor I thought that maybe I was wrong. I thought, 'Well, we'll see.' As a mother you just get that feeling. Anyway, the doctor said to get Lynn playing with more kids.

At that time a new school was opening near by and I thought that would be perfect. I had her around kids. She had played with more kids than her brother had ever played with at that age. But I thought maybe she needed more time with kids. She's a different child. She was just about 28 months old at this time. She went to this program once a week and I expressed to the teacher my concerns about Lynn's language, and again, she told me that each child is different. The teacher said she would keep an eye on it.

'No! There is something wrong!'

By the end of the year, she had made some progress, but it was very slow. Not just in language but other areas, as well. Anything that had to do with music, she led the group. She loved the group setting, but only if it had to do with music time. Otherwise, she had nothing to do with the other children. I thought that she just preferred to play by herself but by the time she turned three I thought, 'No, there is something really wrong.' I went back to the pediatrician and told her that Lynn was putting words together and had been for a year but that she hadn't gone any further. And she was having trouble socializing. How was she going to learn to socialize if she couldn't talk? The doctor thought that maybe something was a little off, but still wasn't too concerned.

'She's not THAT!'

Certainly I wasn't thinking it was autism! In school I had only learned of the most severe. I had a family member who worked at a residence for disabled people and I would help out in the summer. The disabilities were so severe. The autistic people I saw would wander around and bang their heads, make weird noices, sit in the most bizarre pretzel positions, and they looked distorted. To me that was autism. I thought of Lynn, and I thought, 'She's not *that*!' She's a smart kid and there has to be a way to fix that little glitch. Then everything will be okay.

'I was going to fix her'

I was with her day in and day out. But I did think that during the summer, when her brother was at camp, I would have time with just her and I was going to fix this thing. I was going to get her potty trained and I was going to fix her.

That summer she did do well, as long as we were doing what she wanted to do, she was wonderful. She started to name things and was happy to see me. Before that, I wasn't Daddy so it didn't matter if I came into a room. She progressed. That's why I didn't do something sooner because every time I got really crazy with worry she would do something new and I would say to myself, 'Stop! You're making yourself crazy!'

A girlfriend came to visit after that. When we picked her up Lynn didn't look at her. She said, 'Why isn't she looking at me?' and I said, 'She's looking at your hat.' The friend replied, 'But why isn't she looking at my face?' 'So she doesn't like your face, don't take it personally!' I said, 'She's just a different child.' I was angry but I'm grateful that she said something. She had the courage to say something that other people had thought but hadn't said. My brother who had worked with developmentally disabled kids hadn't said anything. He thought it was something, but he didn't think it was autism.

Evaluation

The pediatrician had said that because I was so worried about this thing he would refer me to a speech therapist. It took us six weeks to get to see her and it was a terrible visit. Now that I know autism, Lynn had all the earmark signs; inattentiveness, lack of eye contact, all the language stuff. I mean this is a professional and all she said was: 'I can't test her, she's too uncooperative. She needs to be disciplined.'

She started to tell me how to raise my child. I looked at that. I wasn't pleased with her but I did think about what she said. I had another child who was perfectly fine so it couldn't be my parenting. As we went to leave Lynn said, 'Put your coat on Daddy, let's go!' She had never put a sentence together like that before. I thought, 'Whoa!' We left with mixed emotions. I was committed to spending more time with her. I was going to make the difference.

I don't understand why she (the evaluator) couldn't have said, 'Maybe there's something going on here.' Or, 'You should have her looked at further. I'm having a hard time testing her, but maybe you should go elsewhere.' She was a professional after all.

Our extended family lives a few hours away so we don't see them a whole lot. One time we left the children for a weekend with the family and I was so scared about doing it. But my parents said, 'Oh, she'll be fine, don't worry!' After the weekend they said, 'She listened for us.' And, I thought, 'Did you feed her all day?' That's my mother's thing. My mother said, 'There's nothing wrong with her. She eats!' Lynn connects with her grandfather very well. She seems to love men. So, anyway, the grandparents thought things were fine.

On the home front

Meanwhile, I was trying to keep clothes on her and go shopping. She was awful in the store. She had started this habit of getting up at three o'clock in the morning and taking her clothes off in front of our mirror. Then she would do a Mickey Mouse routine. Every night. It was getting harder and harder. Then again, when I was doing something that she wanted to do she was an absolute delight. I started trying to slip in little stuff that I wanted to do. I finally got her potty trained. It took a week but I did it. Still couldn't get her to read. Except for this one book. *Goodnight Moon!* We had to read it the same way and touched the same pictures. I even had to use the same voice. If I tried to change anything she would have a fit. Or, if I would try to slip in a new book she would say, 'No!' She still wasn't saying 'Mommy' and she referred to herself as 'Lynn' but wouldn't say 'me' or 'I.' She didn't use pronouns correctly.

'The miracle worker'

My husband was still thinking that she was progressing and just needed a little help. By this point I was thinking, 'You come live in my shoes all day long with this.' This is the weirdest thing, but I had this experience one day when I had a flash of *The Miracle Worker*, the story of Helen Keller with Patty Duke and Ann Bancroft, and I thought, 'I'm like Ann Bancroft. There's something really wrong here!' I told myself, 'No, no, no. You're such a drama queen. Get this out of your mind.' But there was that flash.

The summer continued. Lynn was supposed to start nursery school in the fall and I couldn't sleep at night. I would replay the whole day in my head and then wake up my husband. He finally agreed to get more evaluation. I think so that he could get some sleep. I told him, 'If they tell me I'm crazy, that'll be great!' My insides were telling me something was not right and during the day I could work it out of my mind, but at night it was keeping me up. Between that and the nightly visits of Mickey Mouse, I couldn't think straight.

Developmental pediatrician

I called my brother and told him I was terribly worried about Lynn. That's the first time he said to me that he thought there was something wrong. He told me to go to the school district. I didn't want to go to the school so he told me to go to a developmental pediatrician. He told me he knew of one in our area because he had looked around. I wanted to know why he didn't say anything to me sooner. He said, 'Because you didn't ask me.' If he had told me it may have given me the little push that I needed. I think people just thought that she was spoiled rotten. People aren't accepting of a disability when it isn't visible. Here was this beautiful child, with awful behavior. People don't jump to conclusions about the parents when they see a child who looks different. They think there's something wrong with the child, not the parent.

I called to get an appointment with the developmental pediatrician and I told them my concerns on the phone. I asked them if they thought that we needed to come in and they said yes. They had a cancellation the next day and we took the opening.

'Everything stopped'

During the evaluation she did all her little tricks. I still thought it was a little thing. I never realized it was going to be serious. The minute the doctor said the 'A' word (autism), I shut down. I couldn't hear. I thought everything just stopped. I was watching the doctor's mouth move and I knew I needed to listen to this but I just couldn't. Later on I wondered if that is what it's like for Lynn. To be detached in that way. I had never had that kind of experience before. I asked if I could come back with my husband and we arranged for that. I took home information, but I left 'out of it.' On the way home I thought, 'I have to call, I have to call.' So I pulled off the road, got Lynn out of the car and called my husband from one of those phones on the side of the highway. He said, 'So, what did they think?' I told him they said Lynn was autistic. He asked if I was okay and I said, 'No, I'm really not.'

No matter what was going on, we knew Lynn had deficits and we had to get her help. In one sense I thought, 'Okay, I'm not crazy,' and now we have a name for this. I hadn't thought about autism but my gut had been telling me for a while that things weren't right. We returned to the developmental pediatrician for more discussion and we did some reading about the disorder. We did begin to see how Lynn fitted the diagnosis and my husband wanted to investigate further. I wanted to get help for Lynn started.

Shortly after that, I got very angry at all those people who could have identified this sooner. I learned about 'the window of time' (idea that there is a specific period of time when a child is most responsive to intervention) and I felt we had lost time. The doctor was very clear though, and I don't think that they all are, about what we had to do from there. That was helpful. The doctor didn't throw her arms up and tell us to go start checking out institutions. She did say that Lynn was going to need one-on-one supervision and intervention focused on her particular areas of need. She told us that we as parents were going to have to be very involved and follow through on all her training. She told us that there were a lot of good programs out there and that we were going to have to find a program that would work for us. We got the wheels in motion after that visit.

I do remember when it all started to sink in. We were in the car driving and the kids were sleeping. I heard these awful noises and realized that they were coming from me. And, I couldn't stop. I just sobbed. I had the ability though to say, 'I can't do this right now. I *have* to do *this*.'

Finding programming

When I was looking into approaches I just felt that ABA was the only one that really had success with children like Lynn. I couldn't understand how play therapy was going to be different than what I was already doing. She really needed structure and she was in her own little world. I felt that play therapy was going to let her stay in that own little world and not pull her into ours. It went back to making the parents the bad guys because we must not have been playing right if they were going to play differently to help her. This is a neurological disorder and it has to be treated like one.

I called another program and they worked with a lot of disabled kids. They said Lynn would be a good role model for their other students. I wanted Lynn to *have* good role models, not to *be* one.

The program that we did find was very upbeat and optimistic. I thought this was totally nuts, or this was exactly what we needed. I went to see the program. It was hard. The smell was of antiseptic. The whole thing was hard. I looked in the room and it was cheerful. The director took me in a room and asked me to point out which child I thought was autistic. I couldn't guess. I watched this little boy playing, sharing, talking. He was diagnosed autistic six months before. I said, 'Okay. When can we start?'

From there I had to go to the school district. I think I threw myself on the chairman's floor! I cried. I let it go. I said, 'You have to help me!' Until the age of 6 the brain is so incredible. You have to make the difference when the brain can best accommodate. Maybe there are pockets there that we can tap into or circuits that haven't been stimulated. It made sense to me to do a lot during this time and I wanted the school district to agree. I'd do anything to help my kid. The school district agreed to sending Lynn to the program.

We learned the ABA techniques used in the school and did a great deal at home as well. We included activities, such as swimming, into our family life. It was important to us to have a family life as well as spend a good deal of time on training skills for Lynn. It was hard to find time for it all.

We were also concerned about how Lynn's brother was handling all this. After all, this was his sister. At this point she wasn't invading his territory or his toys. I asked another mother how she had explained this to her other children and she told me that she described it to the children as being like having a monster in your head. And, I asked him to help me get rid of that monster. I said to him, 'You know how we have to leave places sometimes because Lynn can't behave, or you can't come in my bed because it would be too upsetting to Lynn. Well, there's an awful monster in Lynn's head and it affects her brain. What we have to do is get that monster smaller. It's not your sister. It's the monster. She doesn't want that monster in her brain.' It seemed to really make sense to him and I found that when she would do something awful, he would say, 'That monster is doing bad things. I don't like that monster.' He asked me how we were going to get rid of the monster. I told him we had to teach her and her good brain cells would get bigger. Later he was sitting with her pointing to a book saying, 'Lynn, this is an apple.' Lynn adores her brother. Sometimes he still says 'Mommy, it's just not fair.' I say, 'You're right. It's just not fair.'

Things can get rough. We have moments. She'll want to wear shorts and a T-shirt and it's snowing outside. She's in a fit while her brother is trying to have breakfast and get the school bus. Fortunately, I have a half hour after she leaves to spend a little time with him. It's tough.

'You have to be an advocate'

Lynn went into a regular kindergarten after two years of special programming. She had the support of an aide, a speech therapist and occupational therapist. The previously used ABA techniques were carried over to the school program. It's your child and above all you know your child better than anybody else. You have to be a major advocate for her. I've always felt that it was my responsibility to raise the child and the teachers are there to help me. They are there to work with me and help to create a fine human being. I've had to keep a close eye on things or things would get shifted around. When they said that they didn't have enough speech therapists I told them to hire another one.

'I want her to be okay'

I just wish I knew how Lynn is feeling because she can't tell me. I hope there is a day that she will be able to tell me how she was feeling at certain times. As her mother, I want to make her feel better. I want her to be okay.

Bobby

Bobby's story is unlike the others in that his parents were not surprised by the diagnosis of Asperger Syndrome but rather were relieved. They had intuitively sensed that something was different about their child and had done quite a bit of research to better understand those differences. The research, and input of others, led them to the diagnosis of Asperger Syndrome before they 'officially' received that label. The process was not an easy one, however, and Bobby's early years were tumultuous times for his family. Bobby's father, Rob, shares his frustrations, challenges, and triumphs in their story.

Early years

Bobby was a very good baby right from the beginning. He was a great eater and a great sleeper. At two months the doctor recommended that we drop his night-time bottle. The next night we didn't go in when he woke in the middle of the night, and we never had to again. At around six months of age he started with ear infections. He had a lot of them and cried a lot. For a while we told ourselves that he had become fussy because of the ear infections. But, we had a feeling, especially Judy, my wife, that something was wrong early on. We didn't talk about it a whole lot back then. We might have said, 'Boy, that seems like something other than an ear infection.' But we didn't really talk about it a lot. We were willing to rationalize his differences at that point.

I can remember times when we went out places or to a family member's house and I was the only one he would let hold him. He wouldn't even let anyone touch him, not even his hands. We thought, 'Oh wow, maybe his ears hurt so much that everything hurts.'

Concerns worsen

Between 1½–2½ years old, we noticed that he was having problems. If we went to someone's house, even a small crowd, he would instantly have problems. When he became mobile, which he did around age one, he wouldn't go off with other kids. He's got several cousins and we would get together and he wouldn't interact with the other kids. All the other kids would be off playing. Bobby would cling to me, or tantrum. That started to bother us. I wasn't too worried at that point because when we were home, he was happy, he seemed okay. He had a large book collection and he would flip through the books by himself. He didn't need someone reading them to him. You could put him next to a pile of books and return in an hour to find the books stacked on the other side of him. He would have looked through each one and he wouldn't have moved. He was happy with it so we didn't make a big deal of it. But, then we got to the point that we would try to push him to go play with the other kids so we could have some time with adults, and he would resist us. Some times he would go but then he would call us in a very short time to come about a little thing that shouldn't have bothered him.

He started talking right on time. If you want specific details you have to talk to my wife. She will know the date, time, and place exactly. As I recall, even around a year he was actually pointing at a tree and saying, 'tee'. He was gesturing and seemed to understand communication. He would do stuff for us at home where he was comfortable that he wouldn't do anywhere else, though. He talked mostly to us.

At home, things were not so out of sorts. Judy was really tuned in though. She sensed something was going on early. I was sort of chalking it up to 'Hey, he's just being shy' or 'He's just quiet.' Judy picked up that it wasn't normal. I have to admit that I was frustrated. On a selfish front I was maybe even embarrassed at times. I thought, 'Why isn't our kid like the rest of the kids?' I wondered if other parents were thinking, 'How are they raising this kid?' When Bobby was content with something, I would stop worrying. It started to bother me more when I felt that Bobby was upset about it too. It was like he wanted to be in there with other kids but he wasn't letting himself go.

Response to wife's concerns

Judy was around Bobby a whole lot more than I was. She had a lot more exposure to him. So, even though I wasn't all that concerned initially, I figured that there had to be something to what she was concerned about. I didn't really communicate that to her so much, it was more to myself. At that point, when she really started to have serious concerns, it was difficult for her to just get through the day and I didn't want to add to those concerns. He had started to be upset easily by minor changes in his routine. It made for a tough day for mom at home with her first child. We spent a lot more time just trying to get through the hours rather than spending much time sitting around talking about it. It was the end of the day when I came home from work and we would just hope that the next day would be better for him.

Judy was able to get into a routine with Bobby that made things manageable. He really did well when things were kept the same. Some days just because I literally walked in the door, I would throw everything off. It would cause the day to swing out of control. I think there was a breaking of the routine. Judy would have a nice equilibrium going, and I would walk in the door and shatter that. Just by walking in the door! Because we only had a couple hours in the evening every day, my routine wasn't to come home like a typical guy and say, 'I'm gonna go home and play with my kid.' He didn't seem to feel comfortable when I came in. That was hard. I was frustrated that I didn't have much time with him. I was frustrated because I knew that Judy's day was hard, and I was making things worse. I was frustrated that I couldn't relate to my son. I was frustrated because I didn't know why I made things worse. It was all very frustrating and difficult to accept. Selfishly, personally, I felt bad for myself, but I felt bad for them too. I felt part of the problem. I felt helpless not knowing what I could do differently. Should I be more strict, or less strict? I was trying everything, knowing nothing.

Diagnosed Asperger Syndrome

Around two and a half Bobby really cut loose at the doctor's office so she finally agreed, for the first time, that something might not be quite right. He tantrummed so bad and was so out of control that she thought maybe there was something to our concerns. She really didn't have any major suspicion but she wanted to rule out anything that might have been major. She thought that maybe he was having seizures so she referred us to a neurologist. The neurologist couldn't really do anything because Bobby was so upset at the first visit that the doctor couldn't even examine him. This was a hard time. When I went to the visits it seemed to make Bobby worse. I wanted to be there, but I knew it was harder for everyone because I was there. Again, I felt like part of the problem and not able to help my own son, and wife. The neurology visit was so bad that we could hardly even talk to the doctor. After that Judy took him to the visits alone. I felt like a bystander, for my own son. I was out of the mix.

At just over two-years-old, we took Bobby to see a psychologist who essentially told us it was about our parenting. Apparently, he felt we needed to be better disciplinarians. That wasn't particularly helpful.

After that, Judy took Bobby to another neurologist. I wasn't at this meeting because we knew it would throw Bobby off. That was hard, to know something was up and that my wife had to go alone. At the same time, we knew it was the right decision. The neurologist was particularly interested in Bobby's symptoms. She was actually enthralled with what she saw. In hindsight, despite the frustrations, difficulties and all that, you could see what a special little kid he was. He was incredibly intelligent, creative, and had a sense of humor, even from a very young age. I think the neurologist saw him as a mix of his strengths and weaknesses. Bobby was a fascinating child. The neurologist threw out the term Asperger's but didn't know too much about it at that point so she referred us to a developmental pediatrician. We both did a lot of reading before that visit and we became pretty confident that Bobby did fit that diagnosis. After we read about the disorder, we definitely saw some of the symptoms of Asperger's but we saw these other things too.

It was given a name

After it was given the name, Asperger Syndrome, we started the research around here. We read everything that we could get our hands on. We would have been surprised if it hadn't been called Asperger's by the time we went to the developmental pediatrician because we had read so much that sounded like Bobby. The idea that it was something that somebody knows about was a relief. Okay, he's not a brat. We're not doing something wrong here as parents. We had gotten many different pieces of advice and people had suggested that it was about our parenting. We felt pretty sure that wasn't the case because we had started seeing problems at such an early age. He had trouble being comforted, or comforting himself as an infant. He had trouble with rigidity of routine as an infant. At some level, we knew it wasn't about us. But, there was a relief in the confirmation of that and in it having a name. We didn't know much about it, but we knew it was something with a name.

There was sadness too. The idea that maybe he was just a difficult toddler, and he's just going to outgrow this was gone. And, the uncertainty of 'What does this really mean?' was unsettling. There were some fears. Overall, I thought, 'Okay, there's something wrong, and there are people out there that we can work with.' I think that up until then we had been floundering. Trying one thing that would seem to work for a while, then all of a sudden it would stop working. We would try something else. He would take to almost anything we would try, for a brief time. After the diagnosis we were able to focus our efforts.

Starting services

After that we went to quite a few places that service children with special needs. They were all different. Some of them actually struck terror in my heart. To see all the levels of disability and to have a child in this arena was very scary. Some classrooms seemed too extreme for Bobby. I don't think that it was denial on our part. We said, 'Okay, he's got this but it's not at the extreme end of the spectrum. It is a part of him but it is not all of him.' We wanted to get him help but we wanted him to get the right kind of help. He was very impressionable. He was a very good mirror. We felt that if he was exposed to severe behavioral disabilities he would mimic those behaviors.

Eventually, we did find a program that we liked very much. There were special needs kids of different levels but it also seemed pretty typical. And, Bobby seemed to immediately fit in there.

Fixations

One of the things about Bobby is that while we know he has Asperger's we also see things about him that don't exactly fit with what we read. Yes, he has fixations but they change over time. They don't stay the same. They last about two to three months and then he gets a new obsession. The first one I remember was when he was just beginning to talk. I taught him the names of the 'Dwarfs' and I could just see his little mind memorizing them. He would say 'Who dat?' And, quickly he knew them all and recited them regularly and in different orders. Then it became trucks, then dinosaurs, that was a big one. Now it seems to be *Pokemon*. He knows way beyond what you would think a kid would know about these things.

I noticed very early that he really enjoys numbers. He loves to count. He got off the school bus the other day and said that he had counted to 500 on the way home. I asked him, 'Five-hundred what?' And he said 'Just five-hundred numbers.' I think it calms him, like whistling or singing would. He does seem to have exceptional skills with numbers. In kindergarten he is doing addition and subtraction. Numbers have been an interest that has persisted throughout all the others. Number concepts are just something that he has always felt really comfortable with. He also loves puzzles. He would do the wooden ones over and over as a little guy. He still can occupy himself for a long time with puzzles.

His social world

Bobby saw his cousins a fair amount and, even though he was comfortable with them, he really wouldn't socialize in a group. He just seemed to have no interest in other kids. School really helped in this area. I could tell from day one at the school that he was going to do better there. At first he held back a little bit but then the teacher came over and he went with her. He went without even much coaxing. I don't know if it was that it was so much of an unfamiliar situation that he just didn't know to be nervous or what. He seemed to join right in. Judy and I watched from the sidelines amazed.

There were all kinds of toys around the classroom and he went to take something off the shelf. The teacher said, 'No, Bobby come play with these.' She directed him to put the toys back and then to join the others with the toys on the floor. Judy grabbed my hand and had tears in her eyes. We thought that he was going to cut loose but he just went with it. That was when the light bulb went off and we knew that the schooling was going to give him something that we couldn't give him. The teacher was so matter of fact in directing him and she knew how to handle him. He settled right into the programming and we almost immediately saw him start to change socially. Right away he wanted to know the names of the other kids in his class and he learned them.

Kindergarten

After the positive preschool programming we decided to put him in regular kindergarten. The only special servicing that he started with there was speech therapy. That was mostly for articulation problems. We also had a monthly consultation with psychology just to keep on top of things. We didn't have direct servicing for Bobby but we didn't want to pull the rug out from under him either. We didn't want to hide the diagnosis. We know that it can manifest itself in different ways at different times, so we are always on the look out. We want the school to be aware too, so we didn't want to hide anything from them. He is doing better than we hoped, mainstreamed with no supports in the regular classroom. The teacher has the diagnosis in the back of her mind but she tells us that he is a delight to have in class. We knew he had come a long way but we were surprised to have him go into regular kindergarten with such little support.

Family and friends' reaction to Asperger's

I think that before the diagnosis people did think that he was different because of the way we were raising him. After the diagnosis was official, everyone (family and friends) came right on board and were very supportive. Until that point I think, in part, that the family might have been in denial and, in part, they thought that we should just 'straighten him out'. Since the diagnosis though, they have all been totally supportive. It has made a big difference.

The future

When I look to the future I am very hopeful. There is concern still. He is only five and as he grows his friends also grow so the social challenges will continue. He is probably never going to be totally free of the Asperger symptoms. We still see a real struggle with the empathy issue. He just cannot see another's point of view or feelings.

In his day-to-day interactions things have to go by his own rules. That is not always going to work in the world and that concerns me. Other kids won't understand that perspective and I'm afraid that he won't fit in. I'm also afraid that he will be ostracized.

Role as father and husband

I don't know so much about the specifics of the dates and times of how all this transpired. Judy knows all the particulars. I didn't feel so much that I was pushed out of the picture. It was more that I felt helpless when I was in the picture. I was more than helpless; I made things worse for my son and wife. I disrupted the routine that was so important to Bobby feeling secure. I felt I let them down in some ways but it wasn't a matter of choice. I did selfishly feel I was playing a different role than most fathers get to play.

The other thing that was hard, was to feel like I had to justify Bobby's behavior. If a child has a disability that you can see, say he is in a wheelchair or blind, no one would question the child's behavior. When children look like other kids but act differently it's hard to explain. There were times I felt I had to justify Bobby's actions. I did feel worse for him, though, than for myself.

Whether having a child with Asperger's makes you stronger or weaker as a couple has to do with what you do with it. At first, Bobby's struggles consumed us. It literally became our life. We tried to keep some of ourselves alive but we weren't very successful at it. It wasn't until we got the diagnosis and started getting the support of the school that we were able to see how consumed we were with Bobby's needs. Once things started to get better for him we realized we needed to live life a little ourselves, and with each other as a couple. If we hadn't realized this, and turned things around, it could have been very destructive.

I have to add that going through this situation with Judy has shown me a lot about her. She was the reason we identified this so early and got him help at such a young age. The strains this may have caused built into a sincere, incredible appreciation of my wife. She has shown me strength that I find amazing!

'Life has treated me well'

I admit that there have been frustrating and embarrassing times as a parent but I have to say that I am incredibly proud of my son. He is not just along for the ride. He is clearly part of the solution. He has put in so much effort and he has made such progress. I remember watching him when he wasn't even three-years-old and he knew that he had done something wrong. It was as if he was watching himself from outside of himself. My pride for him outweighs any possible embarrassment.

I have had a lot go my way in life. Life has treated me well. This really is one of the first challenges to my faith. It definitely has its negative side but so much of our life is still 'silver-lined'. Even with Asperger Syndrome, Bobby is such a special guy. We always saw him that way. There are so many positives and I have a lot of faith in him.

About Christopher

Christopher is an older child with Asperger Syndrome. Like so many children with Asperger's, the collection of his developmental differences didn't spell out any particular disorder until later in his life. Certainly, Jan, his mother, recognized Chris' struggles early on, and she has worked instinctively to help him along his path of growing up. She has sought the support of many professionals throughout his life yet only recently had him diagnosed with Asperger Syndrome. This is their story told by Jan.

Chris was born outside of the United States and was nine weeks premature. He had a life-threatening heart condition and our total focus for his first few years of life was around that. When he was two weeks old he had *apneic* episodes *(periods of not breathing)* and he had an *echo* (*a diagnostic test of heart function*). It was amazing there because they didn't have a lot of medical equipment so they had to be really good diagnosticians. *Chris was treated and had surgery by the age of two.* When he was in the hospital following his surgery I asked for an orthopedic consultation because he wasn't hitting his motor milestones. He didn't roll over, sit up, or start to walk as expected. And, he didn't pursue toys out of reach. My strong intuition told me that there was more to this than just the cardiac stuff. The ortho doctor told me essentially to relax. I was an older mother and he thought that I was over-reacting. My husband had to just about restrain me. I knew something wasn't right. I said, 'Well, I'm going to keep knocking on doors.' This was January and we went back to see him in June. He said 'Yes, there is something wrong.'

We started to look more closely at the other stuff. Chris still could barely hold himself up on a push train. Chris was about 2½ by this time. He was snugly and affectionate. He loved to giggle and laugh. He was very passive and almost placid. He didn't cry a lot and I could always comfort him. I just thought I had an easy baby. He wasn't verbal at all. He had created his own sign language to interpret his world. We took him to church every Sunday and his sign for church was to pat the top of his head. That was what the pastor did on the way out of church. You had to figure out what the signs meant.

Different doctors, different opinions

The pediatrician we were going to at the time had attributed a lot of his delays to the heart problem. We went to a different doctor to look at this further. He told us we needed to get Chris's hearing tested and find out why he was not talking. Everyone said we were older parents and we were doting on him, etc. Anyway, we did have the hearing test done and that was found to be fine. Then we took him to a center for developmental disabilities and had him tested there. They agreed that he was developmentally delayed and we should do some further medical testing to find out why. I guess to make sure it wasn't anything pathological.

At this point we went to a neurologist who said that it looked like cerebral palsy (CP), maybe. He said that it definitely wasn't anything that was regressive because he was improving. He really couldn't come up with anything specific so he labeled it 'CP-like syndrome'. We really didn't want to do any invasive testing. He was only 3 years old.

School starts

We got him into a special school and they found him to be severely speech delayed and they started doing intensive speech therapy. He was getting speech, occupational therapy, and physical therapy very intensively in the classroom. That intervention really got him going. I am so grateful to this school. We still keep in touch with some of them. Anyway, Chris was talking by the fall after one summer program.

I remember after he started to talk it struck me odd that he would always 'parrot' me. Once he started to talk he was just totally verbal. It seemed that all his thoughts were gleaned from other people. It became obvious that he wasn't really initiating his own language. My radar went up. The other thing that I started to notice was that he didn't have a clue about reading other people's emotions. If I were furrowing my brow inquisitively he would think I was mad. He couldn't read normal expressions. In hindsight I can see a lot of that, but at the time I just thought that it was a little unusual.

More oddities emerge

Chris never had tantrums, and stuff that kids just seem to go through, he didn't seem to go through. We had a rectangular coffee table that he used to chew on. I did think that was an extreme kind of thing. Also, if you moved the table, he knew that it wasn't in the right place. Same thing in his room. He didn't want you to change anything because he needed it in order. He would cry and get angry. Change would set him off.

The other piece was that with other kids in the classroom Chris was always the observer, not a participant. He clung to any adult that was near by. He would watch the kids and seem interested. He didn't have a flat affect, but he never got in the fray. You could encourage him but it was always a struggle. You really had to push him. He would throw up, still does, if you force him to do something. From the anxiety I think. One time we went out to dinner and I left him with a sitter. She called us at the restaurant and said that Chris had thrown up. I said, 'Is he breathing?' He was. 'Did you clean it up?'

She had. So what was the problem, I thought. She probably thought that we were terrible but I wasn't going to freak out about this stuff. I thought it was just his anxiety.

Then again, it was out of the realm of what I heard other moms talking about.

Vulnerability and obsessing

Chris does have an engaging way about him but it seems he has a huge sign on his chest that says, 'I'm a victim.' He's not picked on a lot, but kids do seem to pick up on the vulnerability. He's learned enough about socialization now and he wants to be involved. If I have company he always comes down to talk, but it has to be what he wants to talk about.

Chris is obsessed with church. He knows the color of the vestments for the different seasons and can recite the liturgy. He volunteered at the church over the past summer and the pastor thought it best if Chris wasn't there unless both the pastor and the secretary were present. I trust the pastor implicitly but these are the times we live in. This cut down on the time that Chris could be there. I told Chris this rule and he didn't like it. If you tell him a rule in black and white he gets it but it's very hard to describe shades of gray. So then when he went back to school he wanted to know why he could be with other people there alone. What is good is that I'll explain something and he'll chew on it and I know I'll get more questions the next day. I've told him that sometimes people don't know the same rules, sometimes people choose not to follow the rules, and sometimes people bend them. We try to talk about what's fair. Like with the church pastor, he told him that he didn't like the rule and he didn't think it was fair but that he would follow it. He works it through and assimilates it. He really works on this social stuff. Sometimes to the point where I have to say, 'Stop already!'

Perseveration

Chris will perseverate on some topics and I have to stop him or negotiate to talk about it again tomorrow for a certain amount of time. Like with church. He will talk about it for hours. He knew all the words to the entire mass by the age of three. He did a school project on the governing structure of the church. The interest can be a useful thing. When he was worrying about what he would do for the project I said, 'Why don't you do something about the new bishop?' He didn't think they'd let him do that but they did. He did the whole nine yards to accomplish the project and even went in and made a speech.

Change

The hard part was to get him, in the beginning, to understand when things are different. When we went to a different church he just couldn't get why they weren't following the same rules. Chris notices everything. If something is off center or if the shape of something is different. He notices everything. He can pick up music very, very quickly. He can hear it once and know all the words. That is something I've tried to capitalize on. He's in the chorus and the choir. He hears that tune and he's got it perfectly.

Regular school

When he finished his special school he went into a regular kindergarten. Again, he was always in the background. He was an observer. We joined the art museum and signed him up for art classes. We joined the zoo. We joined the science museum and signed him up for those classes. Getting him to participate in that stuff was very tough. And to prepare him to go was so hard. He would be so anxious the first day he would throw up. I tried to be gentle and to calm him. I'd tell him it would be okay. Looking back on it now I see it wasn't quite right. At the time it was subtle stuff and we just thought he was kind of odd.

Fourth grade was a very difficult year. It was two classrooms put together with two teachers. There were 54 kids in one classroom. Chris had orthopedic surgery that year and he was in a wheelchair for 12 weeks. His father had surgery for cancer. Chris was not doing well academically and his male teacher was a threatener and a screamer. I can pretty much count on what Chris says because he remembers verbatim and he over interprets anger. He would come home and cry about stuff the teacher said. The other kids probably went home and forgot it. Chris spent the whole year with his hands folded thinking that if he did that it would be okay. His anxiety just escalated. Homework was a nightmare. Everything that you said to him was interpreted as highly critical. He was crying, not sleeping and he was bombing out academically. On top of that the other kids were maturing socially and he wasn't.

Socially, academically and emotionally he wasn't doing well. We had to schedule his surgery on break because he was so concerned about missing school. My thought process was that I didn't want to make him more anxious, so even with surgery he never missed a day of school. It went okay because he wasn't in pain and he used a wheelchair.

The other woman teacher took my husband aside and said, 'You might want to think about having Chris tested.' She was concerned about the anxiety thing and didn't really know what was going on with him, so she thought that it might be a good idea. This was the first time they approached us on the matter.

On friendship

I do want to comment on something else. We used to have Chris invite friends over to the house and they never reciprocated. Well, we were going to the mountains for our vacation and we had Chris invite a friend. It was awful. Chris retreated. He wouldn't do anything. Wouldn't swim, go out in a boat, nothing. I think it was the change. I alternated between being affectionate and angry. I would tell him this was unacceptable behavior and he would say, 'Okay Mom, I'll try.' He put this phony face on and I could tell he was struggling. I wanted him to knock it off. He had been so excited about the friend coming and talked and talked about it. On the car ride up they were okay. I don't know what it was, I can't even speculate, but that first night he shut down. We probably should have sought counselling when we got back from the lake but we didn't and he went right into that tough fourth-grade school year.

Concerns re-emerge

We attributed so much of it to his other medical problems. We did start putting these unusual behaviors together. We became more concerned particularly after the teacher approached my husband. This time we went to see a social work/counsellor. We described what was going on and he said to get Chris out of the school setting. So we put him in a private school and decided to delay any testing until he was in the new school for a semester to see how much of what was going on was related to the environment he was in.

At the end of that first semester he was a lot calmer and less anxious. Those teachers approached us and said, 'Let's test him just the same.' So, he was tested that next winter. That testing came up with the diagnosis of a *non-verbal learning disability*. That was very, very vague. I had a friend who is a special educator and I showed her the report to help me interpret it. She agreed it was too vague and suggested another evaluation site. (The friend suggested a site that is familiar with autistic disorders, but Jan did not know that at the time.) We took him to yet another school and had him tested again. During this time his anxiety was worsening. We reviewed all this stuff and three quarters of the way through the conversation they said, 'I think this is Asperger Syndrome.' The evaluator never used the term autism.

'Now we could do something'

My quest all along has been to get this thing identified correctly and then to work with it. I'm not happy about the diagnosis. Do I wish he was normal? Yes! But reality is not going to go away. We actually were glad of the diagnosis and it made sense. Now we could do something about this.

After that we read and networked. We gathered all kinds of information. I'm not yet satisfied that he's had the best workup that he could have had. I feel like I've been going by the seat of my pants. I took him for another evaluation with a school psychologist last summer and that report said Pervasive Developmental Disorder, NOS (not otherwise specified) with an anxiety disorder.

Chris still prefers not to interact with his peers for the most part. He volunteers to clean the cafeteria and school rooms instead of going to the playground. He gravitates toward the odd kids. I was real concerned when my husband died because he didn't seem to have any emotional response to it. I don't know if he had a minimal response or if he has buried his feelings. It worries me.

The future and hope

I think about the future a lot. I get scared and depressed. I also remain hopeful. More than one person has said that he will be able to go to college. Society is more ready for different people. This is 1997 not 1947. Is it going to be a struggle? Yes.
I know that he is here for a reason. I have a deep faith and trust in God. He will watch over Chris. He has this far! I also think that Chris can accomplish something significant. He has touched our lives in positive ways. He is a wonderful person!

About Luke

Ellen stood at the doorway. Her initial greeting was proceeded by an exhaustive sigh. Introductions were made and her tension visibly cleared as she settled on the couch beside a tray of tea. We began the interview after an informal chat. Ellen had a great desire to share the story of her four-year-old son, Luke. It was apparent that this woman had a very 'full plate' yet it was important to her to take time to share her story. And, share she did.

'The bottom fell out that year!'

Between September and October, as Luke approached his second birthday, he developed a series of ear infections that lasted for a year. With the ear infections came a total loss of language. Before that time he had words. He became progressively more irritable and weepy, and it seemed his behavior worsened when he was on antibiotics. He was also on antibiotics from October to May. He lost skills and knowledge that I knew he had. He was still able to do simple puzzles and was particularly adept at shape sorting. Up until that point he was a very cheerful, happy child. At least that is what I perceived. The bottom fell out that year!

Once the ear infections had cleared up and Luke was off antibiotics, he was not the same child. We noticed that he spaced out a lot, would not stay on task, especially on table top activities. He wouldn't be able to do even simple things like painting. He started to do bizarre things like trying to eat the paint or run the paint brushes through his hair. All he wanted to do was sit in the corner with his car and spin the wheels.

When he stopped responding to his name being called we thought that he had a hearing problem. We were assured by his doctor and family members that he'd be better. Blah, blah, blah! I was concerned about the loss of language and I was told that he was jealous of other kids in the daycare I had started in my home. Luke started talking around the time he was one year old. Maybe he had about 20 words but then he just stopped using them. He would shriek to communicate what he wanted.

'There we were supporting each other's denial'

Looking back on it now, I can see that there were peculiarities even in infancy. Even at one month. I breast fed, and I noticed that he preferred to look at the wall instead of me. I had read about that being a sign of early autism. Ironically, my husband came home one day when I was crying and I told him of my concern about this. He said, 'Oh, that's okay. One of our neighbors was saying exactly the same thing.' At the time those were reassuring words. Well, the neighbor's child is now diagnosed with Asperger's! There we were supporting each other's denial. Our children were doing the same things.

Luke was extraordinarily sensitive to sound. He could not tolerate a lullaby. I had to sing him Beatles songs to sooth him, but lullabies, like 'Twinkle, Twinkle, Little Star' and 'Mary had a Little Lamb' would send him from the room crying hysterically. We just figured he was sensitive. He did like people. He cuddled. It was just that his eye contact was poor and that his hearing was sensitive. Now, we were a new mom and dad, and we didn't know what any of this meant. We knew that he liked to cuddle with us and his grandparents.

Then I started taking other kids in for daycare and he didn't seem to like them. He liked older children but not his peers. He followed the older kids around and would inappropriately grab on to them. Even that degree of socialization decreased over time.

'I was not a good mother'

Luke was having problems because I was not a good mother. That was a pretty universal opinion of friends and family. I was pushing him too hard. I wasn't pushing him hard enough. Some family members said it was because I was playing Disney movies and the violence in them was what was disturbing him. So I was supposed to believe that it was because he watched *Beauty and the Beast* that he had behavior problems. That's why he wouldn't sit down or paint? That was the reason he just ran around without direction, because he was disturbed from the movie?

Others suggested that it was something in his diet so I took just about everything out of his diet. Then it was just that I worry too much, or that I was too nervous. I had some serious moments of insecurity.

Once Luke got the diagnosis it seemed to immediately lift some weighted burden that rested on my shoulders. Everybody got off my back. I think my husband apologized on behalf of his family for their notion that I was too nervous and I was damaging Luke. They all have come to realize now that I had extraordinary demands on me.

By this point I had a colicky infant, Luke's new brother, and Luke with his difficulties. I recall that every day was utter hell for me. There was great satisfaction in saying, and knowing, 'It's not because of me!'

Who initially became concerned?

I was the one most concerned initially and my mother after that. My husband had some concerns but he thought that Luke would outgrow them. The pediatrician was also very concerned. On Luke's second birthday, when I told her that Luke had lost language, the doctor referred us to the county for early intervention. That was, as I explained before, at a point at which I wasn't ready to accept anything serious was wrong.

After he was evaluated at 25 months of age, the evaluators said that he was functioning at about the 11-month level. I knew inately that my kid had a lot of smarts. I guess my denial kicked in and I assured myself that he was not that bad. I didn't understand. They were very nice and all, but I didn't think that they took into account that a child can vary from day to day and that they weren't able to get him to do things that I had been able to get him to do that previous summer. I didn't realize what we were looking at and that the loss of those skills was highly significant. Nobody spelled that out to me.

The evaluators wanted to do more testing. I told them that I thought it was a speech problem and that I really didn't think I wanted to do anything yet, in terms of initiating intervention services. They asked if they could come back in six months. I remember the two examiners looking at each other. I didn't understand the significance of those glances. Now I do.

The examiners called six months later and wanted to come to see him again. I was in a full blown depression by then brought on by the stresses of taking care of Luke, taking care of other kids, and the criticism from others. It was not appropriate that I didn't respond to the phone messages, or follow up on getting more testing. It was just that I did not want to hear one other person call me a lousy mother.

'It's not you! It's your child!'

A few months after that I went to a birthday party. I was speaking to the mother of the child who was having the party. She was watching Luke and she was watching me. Finally she approached me and asked, 'How are things going with Luke?' We began to talk and I started to share everything. She said, 'You know I'm a single mother with two girls and I don't work as hard as you on your one boy.' She was being very sweet. 'Does your pediatrician know?' I continued to tell her the whole story. She encouraged me to call my pediatrician again. 'Ellen, it's not you! It's your child! You didn't do anything wrong.'

Some time after that encounter, I found out that the woman at the party worked with disabled people and knew about autism. She knew the signs and she had been so sweet to me. She approached me and she did it the right way. She said, 'It's not you!' I bless her. She was the first voice that was not critical.

The waiting game

Then it was the waiting game. I didn't realize I could have had him seen through an urgent visit, but instead we waited two months for the next available appointment with the pediatrician. I explained everything to him. He was astonished that Luke was not getting services. 'Did you call the county? You've got to call the county right away!'

I called the county when he was almost 35 months old. They informed me that they couldn't get out to see Luke until after his third birthday and that meant that we had to call the local school district to get Luke evaluated again. The local school district couldn't get out until after the holidays. From August until January it was just the waiting game.

'Don't you think he's odd?'

The person from the preschool finally came. It turned out to be the same psychologist who had evaluated Luke before. When she saw Luke she looked shocked. Her mouth dropped open. It was January and Luke was lying down on the wet pavement running his cars back and forth. His shirt had rolled up so his belly was flat against the cold pavement. When I had tried to get him up, he had screamed so I just let him be. She said, 'Don't you think he's odd?' and I said, 'Yes.' (A simple answer that had been long in coming.) 'I'm so glad that you're telling me this because I've been thinking he was odd all year and everyone told me he was just being a kid,' I said. I was so glad she agreed that it was odd because I felt like I was living in this unreality.

Eventually we got Luke inside and attempted to continue on with further evaluation. The psychologist watched Luke as he ate some cereal. He was shoveling it into his mouth with his hands. 'Does he do this all the time?' she asked. I said, 'Yes, but I've been told not to pressure him to use a spoon.' I think she had to make sure that I wasn't a negligent mother. I needed to hear that I wasn't an over-worrying mother.

At that time, the psychologist was very concerned, very sweet and very sympathetic to me. When she was leaving she said, 'He definitely qualifies for special preschool and I want to put him in for more evaluation.' I asked her what she thought he had. She responded, 'I don't know. I'm not a medical doctor. It may be PDD.' I asked her what that was and when she said that it was on the autistic spectrum, I could have thrown up! 'Don't tell me that!' was all I could say.

The word autism

When I thought of autism all that came to mind were kids banging their heads against the wall. This psychologist was the first one to use that word, AUTISM! When I look back on it, I wish that *the word* had been used earlier because it put the fear of God in me. Maybe every parent is different but because people (*referring to professionals*) were busy trying to protect my feelings, what they really did was delay Luke from getting services. I hadn't realized the importance of getting him services right away. Nobody told me of the significance of lost skills and that is very important. I think that people were putting the focus on me, and my mothering, and not on Luke.

Luke was approved for services through the school district and he entered school in March.

'It can't be! He loves his cat!'

We went to see a developmental pediatrician. That was terrible. We were just put off by her manner. She was very harsh and went straight to the point without giving us enough background. She didn't acknowledge any of his skills and she made it a very black and white issue. This doctor did not look at this as a spectrum disorder and felt that our son was not even playing like a one-year-old. One productive thing did come from the visit though, and that is that she directed us to *ABA (applied behavioral analysis)*. It was a little scary that this doctor thought that this was the only method that would give our son a chance at recovery. She did say that he was not retarded but that he was very socially and verbally impaired and in need of a lot of help. This visit had a big impact on us and we didn't waste any time in getting him into a program from that point, however, we still weren't really accepting of the diagnosis because it wasn't presented as a disorder of varying degrees. Luke didn't fit their image of what is meant to be autistic. Luke was not aloof and he liked to be touched. When he wanted to be left alone we thought it was because demands were being made of him and that he was extremely stubborn. He certainly did things on his own terms! Luke loves his family and grandparents. When he sees his grandfather's car he runs out to it. On the basis of those things, I rejected the diagnosis. He even loves his cat!

'She wore on us like water on a stone'

We had to wait until May for another opinion. Between March and May, Luke started to do some bizarre behaviors. He started walking on tip toes, arching his back, and had weird posturing and facial expressions. He also started to bang his head. By the time we went in May, I was getting an average of two to three hours sleep a night and was severely sleep deprived. I didn't even want to drive the car.

Besides watching the changes in Luke's behavior, the family social worker at the school wore on us like water on a stone to get us to accept the diagnosis. Luke wasn't progressing and was actually regressing. He needed to go into one-on-one therapy and needed the diagnosis or he wasn't able to get that. His therapists were using ABA techniques and they felt he needed more. But we had to accept it first. The family therapist kept calling and kept repeating what she was observing. In May, she started explaining the options for servicing and by the time we went to the second opinion visit, we had accepted the need for the diagnosis.

Luke was higher functioning during the second exam. This doctor is the one who laid it out as a spectrum. The doctor emphasized Luke's loss of skills. He really discussed his play and how he was occupied only for a little while, and that it doesn't progress. He goes on to something else too quickly. Kids over three won't just drop something. The imagination world kicks in and they go into their own fantasy world. This doctor's approach was easier to take. And, we were more ready for the information.

Coping with 'a whole new world'!

I, to be perfectly honest, have been seriously depressed since Luke's birth. There have been periods of elevation. At times my depression was replaced with trying to learn as much as I could. I was driven by a lot of anger at that point. The depression lifted for a couple of months then it settled back in heavily until recently.

When I was younger I had trouble with depression. It is in my family. This is a personal point of mine. In the literature a lot of people will say, in a detached way, that autism correlates heavily with a family history of depression and other conditions like obsessive-compulsive disorder. But then when you're actually working with the professionals, it doesn't seem to be a recognized factor and it's not discussed. They aren't recognizing that parents themselves might be suffering from some of these things and it's going to have an impact on how they handle this. In my own work I always followed the idea that you 'mother the mother' so that she can be a good mother. I think that when one is dealing with parents who may be carrying some of these traits (*such as depression or OCD*) this needs to be taken into account. All this information is coming at you, like how to teach him to potty train, and every little step you're going to follow, and how you're going to reinforce him. Meantime, you've got a whole package inside you. All these intense emotions inside you and you have to learn this whole new way of teaching, this whole new way of parenting, this whole new way of living, this whole new way of structuring your life.

I eventually sought professional help. I tried medications but found them too energy zapping at a time when my child was particularly physically demanding. I could not afford to lose energy. Now I deal with it by talking to other parents. It's really important to know that it didn't just happen to you. It happens to a lot of people. Also, I realized that I needed to take care of myself. I was totally spent. Now, I try to take selfish advantage of any time to myself. I blast music loud and sing. I also do solitary stuff quietly because I have to talk and talk to my son. I garden, read, quiet things.

The emotions are so powerful! I tried to get back in touch with my religious upbringing and make some peace with God as I picture him. I see my child as a sick child. I see my child as a child who has brain damage. He can recover from it by tapping in to other areas of the brain that aren't damaged. Any time that a parent has a sick child, or a hurt child, the emotions are very powerful. If you've been battling depression your whole life and you choose to have a child it is an act of faith. You say I'm going to take this chance. I'm going to prove that life is worth living and then this is done to you. That's how you feel. That it hasn't just been done to your child, it's been done to you. And, you knew all along that God didn't love you. That's how I felt. How can a merciful God do this to this little child? In the meantime, everyone around you is talking very rationally about what to do and you're just swirling with emotions. You have to package the emotions and put them to the side so that you can do what needs to be done for the child. The time is about them, not you. But the suffering is very real. The depression is very real. A professional could help in the healing process by acknowledging this.

The spouse

My husband's defenses and my own went down at the same time. We've been fortunate in that we were in the same place at the same time and agreed on what to do. Otherwise, it would have been hellish. I'm the one who is at home doing the teaching and my husband realizes this. He recognizes that Luke does as well as I'm doing. The sleep deprivation has been hard. My husband will do extra housework. He's been supportive. We also have respite and that's good. His parents babysit sometimes. Luke's whole life is behavioral intervention so it's hard for someone else to care for him. It's all directed activity or drills. Our whole life is around that. Luke has made a lot of progress so it's been worth every minute of it. We've gone from a child who was head banging to one who is verbal.

'He's like a little boy!'

Luke now asks all sorts of questions. He has better associations. He saw the snow blower and said, 'Snow comes soon. Then it's Christmas.' He's starting to learn more easily and he's generalizing information. His language is just starting to have melody. It's not just flat. Intonation is lovely. It's worth it. It's a hell of a way to live, but it's worth it. He's more like a little boy.

'He enters our world!'

I want him to stop being autistic. The first year sometimes I'd take him to his room and then collapse in the middle of the living room floor because I was so totally exhausted and overwhelmed. Feeling alone, so angry. We're trying to make our children like other human beings. I want my son to listen to the songs I love and get up to dance. That has been part of my own behavioral therapy, to show him dancing. My husband loves to ski so we're teaching him to ski. It thrilled us when he saw the snow and said he wanted to ski. This is our reinforcement: when our child enters our world.

Diet

I believe that these children are physically compromised in ways that we do not yet understand. I believe in a special diet for my particular child. At first it didn't seem that the diet was working and he actually had worsened tantrums. Then miraculously his speech just took off.

Every component helps a little bit and when orchestrated together we saw a big change. We see his diet and treatments as supportive of his intervention but not in place of intervention. His ABA is critical for him.

How do we feel about his progress?

There are times I don't know where we are. There are so many areas of concern and it's hard to keep focused on those. Then out of the blue self-stimulating behaviors keep coming back. They increase, they decrease. You talk about the spectrum disorder and some days they fall here, some days there. Overall I know he's made good progress. As parents, what we need is the input from the professionals to help us keep a reality check. We're too close to it every day.

Looking to the future

I try not to think long term, because it scares the dickens out of me. I think about today and tomorrow and maybe next year. I don't think any further than that because I don't know what we'll be looking at. I know what we're hoping for. I hope we're looking at college. It's like a tight rope and I just have to focus on the next step. I've got to focus on what we've got to do today.

I think about the future and I pray. The 'faith factor' is the only thing that keeps my sanity because if I kept hating God I would not have been able to function. I need to believe that there is a higher plan. I need to believe that we're being tested to see exactly what we're made of and I can't ask why God did this to this little child. I need to think that Luke was a soul that was to exist here. There are trials of misfortune and trials of fortune through Luke. We all carry burdens. It's how we carry them that matters.

'Faith factor'

You have to decide which side you're on when times are hard. You have hard decisions to make. There are a lot of personal dreams and wants that you could be pursuing right now, and society would not be judging you too hard. I've had to ask, 'What is the right thing to do?' I didn't agonize over my decision. To stay with him was the only decision because it was the right one. I could be working outside the home and making a lot more money but who would do what I do for Luke? I mean, yes, I want to go swimming, and I want to go to lunch. But, not if it's at a cost to Luke.

When Luke was first diagnosed I felt rage at God inside. It was an act of faith for me to have a baby and I felt let down. I thought I want nothing to do with a God that lets these things happen to children. The only way I could deal with it was to think that this soul of Luke made a choice to be here. All I can figure is that we have lessons to learn from him and through him. It's not that my husband and I are are bad people and therefore need to be tested. We are all tested. It's just that we are being tested in a very overt way. People who have great fortunes are tested by people who are less fortunate. Their tests may be harder because it's so easy to ignore. Maybe we're actually fortunate because our tests are overt and the answers more clear cut. For example, if I had typical children maybe I'd be working full time and not spending the time with them. I might miss their childhood in the flurry of day-to-day, as I see happening in some families. I mean their kids are okay, maybe they are growing up a little too fast though. I don't regret my choice to be with my child at all.

'I wish I followed my instincts!'

Looking back I wish I had been more attentive at the first evaluation. I wish I had followed my instincts and gotten early intervention sooner. I feel pretty guilty about that. But since we accepted the diagnosis I think we've made good decisions for Luke.

Final comments

Programs are individualized and what works for one child might not work for another. This is super important. If a parent hears from other parents that they did something with their child, parents need to go back to their therapists and talk about the idea and possibility of working that into the child's plan. I think it's great to go on line, talk to other parents. But you have to look at the information critically for the individual child. Parents need to look to the specialists for support and work together. The kids need to learn how to '*be*'!

Resources

Books for General Review

Attwood, T. (1998) *Asperger's Syndrome.* London: Jessica Kingsley
 Publishers.
This book is a guide for both parents and professionals. It looks more
specifically at the diagnosis of Asperger's Syndrome and thoroughly
answers frequently asked questions.

Frith, U. (ed) (1991) *Autism and Asperger Syndrome.* Cambridge:
 Cambridge University Press.
This book reviews Dr Asperger's reports and addresses the characteristics
associated with PDD.

Grandin, T. (1986) *Emergence, Labeled Autistic.* Novato, CA: Arena Press.
Written by an adult diagnosed with autism as a child, this book offers
insight into the personal experience and perceptions of an individual with
autism.

Harris, S. (1994) *Siblings of Children with Autism.* Bethesda, MD:
 Woodbine House.
This book is a guide for families and deals with the issue of addressing
autism in siblings and within family structure.

Siegal, B. (1996) *The World of the Autistic Child.* Oxford: Oxford
 University Press.
This book reviews autism as a spectrum and offers treatment resources.

Relevant Publishing Sources

Jessica Kingsley Publishers, London, England

This publisher provides many books related to PDD. Personal accounts of
Donna Williams and others may be helpful in understanding individual
perspectives. Other titles look more closely at treatment and intervention
options.

Future Horizons, Arlington, Tx, USA

This publishing house has multiple titles related to PDD and its surrounding issues.

Educational Materials

Frost, L. and Bondy, A. (1994) *The Picture Exchange Communication System, Training Manual.* Cherry Hill, NJ: Pyramid Educational Consultants, Inc.
This manual reviews utilization of PECs.

Greenspan, S. and Wieder, S. (1998) *The Child with Special Needs.* Reading, MA: Addison-Wesley.
This book looks at the specific methodology of its authors.

Mannix, D. (1993) *Social Skills Activities for Special Children.* West Nyack, NY: Center for Applied Research in Education.
Illustrations and cartoons assist with the social skills training of children.

Maurice, C., Green, G. and Luce, S. *Behavioral Interventions for Young Children with Autism.* Austin, TX: Pro-Ed Inc.
This book outlines the use of applied behavioral analysis as applied to the autistic population.

Koegel, R. and Koegel, L. (1995) *Teaching Children with Autism.* Baltimore, MD: Brookes Publishing Co.
This book reviews helpful strategies for intervention.

Web Sites

www.asperger.org/
www.autism-resources.com/
www.autism-society.org/
www.futurehorizons-autism.com/
www.info.med.yale.edu/chldstdy/autism.com/
www.nih.gov/
www.udel.edu/bkirby/asperger
www.unc.edu/depts/teacch/

References

American Psychiatric Association. (1994) *Diagnostic and Statistical Manual of Mental Disorders* (4th edn.). Washington, DC: American Psychiatric Association.

Frith, U. (ed) (1991) *Autism and Asperger Syndrome.* Cambridge, Great Britain: Cambridge University Press.

Frost, L. and Bondy, A. (1994) *The Picture Exchange Communication System, Training Manual.* Cherry Hill, NJ: Pyramid Educational Consultants, Inc.

Greenspan, S. and Wieder, S. (1998) *The Child with Special Needs.* Reading, Massachusetts: Addison-Wesley.

Lewine, J. D., Andrew, R., Chez, M., Patil, A., Devinsky, O., Smith, M., Kanner, A., Danvis, J., Funke, M., Jones, G., Chong, B., Provencal, S., Weisend, M., Lee, R. and Orrison, W. (1999) Magnetoencephalographic patterns of epileptiform activity in children with regressive autism spectrum disorders. *Pediatrics 104,* 405–418.

Maurice, C., Green, G. and Luce, S. (1996) *Behavioral Intervention for Young Children with Autism.* Austin, Texas: Pro-Ed, Inc.

Mesibov, G.B. (1994) A comprehensive program for serving people with autism and their families: The TEACCH model. In J.L. Matson (ed.) *Autism in Children and Adults: Etiology, Assessment, and Intervention.* Belmont, CA: Brooks and Cole. (pp.85–97).

Index

Alex 29–30
alternative therapies
    107–9
Amy 68
anticonvulsants 84
antidepressants 83–4
anxiety disorders 25–6
Applied Behavioural
    Analysis (ABA)
    92–4
aptitudes 18
Asperger, Hans 28
Asperger Syndrome (AS)
    22, 26–9
    communication
        impairment 51–2
    key characteristics 33
    parents' stories
        123–4, 127
    play impairment 59
associations 54
Attention Deficit
    Hyperactive
    Disorder (ADHD)
    22, 25
attention/impulse
    control 83
autism 29–30
    communication
        impairment 53
    key characteristics 34
    parents' stories
        113–14, 141
autistic spectrum 30

blood work 75
board meeting,
    communication
    48–9
Bobby 120–9
books 149
brain, motor skills 65–6

carbamazepine 84
Chelsea 57, 58
child psychiatrists 72
childhood psychosis 30
Christopher 129–36
chromosomal testing 75
clonidine 83
clumsiness 65
common medications
    82–4
communication 47–56
    assistance 105–6
    definitions 53–5
    early 49–50
    frequently asked
        questions 55–6
    impairment, spectrum
        of 23, 51–3
    learning language
        50–1
    non-verbal 47–9
communication
    augmentation 97
computers, use of 106
concerns, parents' stories
    113, 121–3, 135,
    139
concrete thinking 54–5
connectedness
    communication 51
    development of
        relationships 42

testing 74
continuous EEG 76
control 65–6
conversation, inability to
    initiate 55
cooperative play 41
coordination 65–6
coping, parent's story
    143–4

dance therapy 109
denial, parent's story
    137–8
development see social
    development;
    typical development
developmental delay 21
developmental disorders
    21–2
developmental history
    74
developmental nurses 73
developmental
    pediatricians
    parents' stories
        116–17, 142
    role 72
dextroamphetamine 83
Diagnostic and Statistical
    Manual of Mental
    Disorders 28
diagnostic terminology
    13, 22–3, 30
diet, parent's story 146
diet management 109
differences
    in personality 20–1
    in physical
        appearance 75
discrete trial training
    92–3

disorders
  developmental 21–2
  mistaken for PDD
    76–7
dysmorphisms 75

echolalia 28, 54, 55
educational material
  150
educational treatment
  87–106
  communication tools
    105–6
  educators and
    therapists 90–2
  getting started 87–9
  methods 92–102
  school 102–5
  use of computers 106
educators 90–2
electroencephalogram
  (EEG) 76
Elizabeth 19–20
emotion based
  intervention 96–7
emotionality 19–20
environmental influence,
  social development
  43
evaluation
  ABA 93–4
  disorders mistaken for
    PDD 76–7
  expectations 73–4
  identifying need for
    71–2
  labeling, avoiding 77
  parent's story
    114–15, 117–18
  physical examinations
    75–6

of progress 100–1
  specialists 72–3
evaluators
  experience in
    evaluation 74
  finding 72
eye contact 45

facial expressions,
  infants' response to
  38
factual recitations 54
faith, parent's story 147
fathers, parent's story
  128
Federal Drug
  Administration
  (FDA) 108
fixations, parent's story
  125–6
flexibility, in rules 103
fluoxitine hydrochloride
  84
fluvoxamine maleate 84
fragile X syndrome 75,
  77
friendship, parent's story
  134–5
future, parents' stories
  127–8, 136, 146

gait 66
generalization, ABA 94
Greenspan intervention
  96–7

health food stores 108
hearing 56
High Functioning
  Autism (HFA) 27
holding therapy 109

home front, parent's
  story 115–16
hope, parent's story 136
husbands, parents'
  stories 128, 145
hyperactivity 83
hyperlexia 24, 68

impairment
  communication 51–3
  play style 57–61
  range of 23
  social 39–40, 44
implementation, of
  therapy 97–8
impulse control 83
inability to make
  appropriate openers
  55
infants
  communication
    49–50
  parent's story 120–1
  social development
    38–0
information, quest for
  109–10
instincts, parent's story
  147
interactive play skills 41
Internet
  surfing 109–10
  web sites 150
interventions see
  educational
  treatment; medical
  treatment

John 26–7

Kanner, Leo 30

kindergarten, parent's
    story 127
knowledge, depths of
    25

labeling
    avoiding 77
    parent's story 124–5
    PDD (NOS) 32–3
language
    Asperger Syndrome
        28
    in classrooms 103
    impairment 23
    learning 50–1
    slowness in
        development 55
    use of, out of context
        55
Laundau Kleffner
    syndrome 76
Lovaas methods 92
Luke 136–47
Lynn 112–20

magnetic resonance
    imaging (MRI)
    75–6
magnetoencephalography
    (MEG) 76
mannerisms, physical
    24, 66–7
Mary 19
medical testing 75–6
medical treatment
    79–85
    before starting 81–2
    common medications
        82–4
    considerations 80
    mood swings 80

secondary diagnoses
    79–80
specific medications
    85
memory skills,
    exceptional 24–5
methylphenidate 83
mood stabilization 80,
    84
mothering, parent's
    story 138
motor skills
    alteration in 65–6
    at school 104
movement therapy 109
musical skills, advanced
    25

natural substances 108
Net see Internet
neurologic centers,
    motor skills 66
non-verbal
    communication 39,
    47–9
nonconventional
    treatments 109

observation, ABA 93
obsessions, parent's
    story 132
Obsessive Compulsive
    Disorder (OCD) 25
    antidepressants 83–4
occupational therapists
    73, 91
oddity, parents' stories
    131–2, 140–1
onion peel approach 80
opinions, parents' stories
    130, 142–3

optimal functioning
    language skills 56
    play style 61
    social reciprocity 46

painting time 47–8
parallel play 41
parents, stories 111–47
PDD (NOS) 22
    example of 30–2
    key characteristics
        33–4
    labeling 32–3
pediatric neurologists 72
peer relationships 41
perception 64–5
perseveration, parent's
    story 132–3
personality
    differences in 20–1
    effect on development
        18–20
Pervasive
    Developmental
    Disorder (PDD)
    alternative therapies
        107–9
    characteristics 63–9
    communication
        impairment 49,
        52–3
    defined 22–5
    development of
        relationships
        42–5
    diagnostic
        terminology 13
    disorders mistaken for
        76–7
    educational treatment
        87–106

evaluation 71–7
medical treatment
    79–85
play impairment
    57–61
quest for information
    109–10
social impairment
    39–40
social setting example
    35–8
see also PDD (NOS)
Peter 35–7
physical contact 45
physical examinations
    75–6
physical mannerisms 24,
    66–7
physical therapists 73,
    91
Picture Exchange
    Communication
    System (PECS) 97
play setting, special
    education 94–5
play skills, interactive 41
play style
    frequently asked
        questions 61
    impairment
        example of 58–9
    spectrum of 23,
        59–61
    preference for playing
        alone 45
    typical development
        57
pragmatic disorder 53–4
precipitating factors 81
programs

parents' stories
    118–19, 125
    selecting 99–101
    uniqueness of 101
progress
    developmental 17–18
    evaluation of 100–1
    parent's story 146
pronoun reversal 54
prosody, unusual 28, 55
psychologists 73, 91–2
psychostimulant drugs
    83

qualitative differences,
    in development
    23–4
questions, frequently
    asked
    communication 55–6
    play style 61
    social reciprocity
        45–6

Randy 58–9
reading skills 24, 68,
    104
reciprocal play 41
recitation 54
refrigerator mother 30,
    40
relationship based
    intervention 96–7
relationships
    development with
        PDD 42–5
    early development
        40–2
repetition, in play 61
resources 149–50
reversal of meaning 54

rhythmic movements 67
rules, fixation on 103

Sam 11–12
schizophrenia,
    childhood 30
school
    parent's story 131,
        133–4
    PDD 89, 102–5
secondary diagnoses
    25–6
    medication 79–80
secretin 85
Selective Serotonin
    Reuptake Inhibitors
    (SSRIs) 83–4
self-stimulating
    behaviours 24
semantic disorder 53
sensory perceptions,
    altered 24, 63–4
separation anxiety 38,
    40
sequencing, in play 61
sertraline 84
services, educational
    treatment 89, 90–2
shyness 19
skills
    innate abilities 18
    unusual 24–5, 68–9
    see also motor skills;
        play skills;
        reading skills;
        social skills
sleep disorder 26
social acceptance
    parent's story 126–7
    in school 104–5

social adaptation
      intervention 95–6
social development
      continuing process of
            42
      first and second year
            38–9
      PDD 40, 42–5
social functioning,
      optimum level 46
social impairment 23,
      39–40, 44
social interactions,
      Asperger Syndrome
      28–9
social reciprocity 35–46
social rules
      awareness of 41–2
      children with PDD
            43
social skills
      PDD 35–8
      teaching 43–5
social workers 73, 91–2
spatial awareness, motor
      skills 66
spatial relations 68–9
special education, play
      setting 94–5
special educators 73, 91
specialists
      roles 72–3
      selecting 98–9
spectrum disorder 22,
      23
speech pathologists 73
speech therapy 90–1
stereotypic movements
      24, 66–7
stories, parents' 111–47

strengths, unusual 24–5,
      68–9
support groups 110
symbols, understanding
      50

tactile defensiveness 63
tantrums, parent's story
      112–13
TEACCH 96
temperamental qualities
      child development
            19–20
      social skills 44
testimonials 107
therapists
      roles 72–3, 90–2
      selecting 98–9
thumbsucking 67
Tom 30–2
tone, unusual 28, 55
toys
      fascination with one
            aspect 61
      playing with the same
            61
treatment see educational
      treatment; medical
      treatment
typical development
      17–22, 57, 58

unspoken rules 43
unusual prosody 28, 55
unusual strengths 24–5,
      68–9
unusual tone or volume
      55
use of language out of
      context 55

valproate 84
vulnerability, parent's
      story 132

waiting game, parent's
      story 140
web sites 150
World Wide Web 109